RIGHT ON CUE

RIGHT ON CUE

•AN AUTOBIOGRAPHY•

JOHN PARROTT

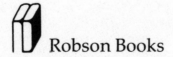

Robson Books

First published in Great Britain in 1991
by Robson Books Ltd, Bolsover House,
5–6 Clipstone Street, London W1P 7EB

British Library Cataloguing in Publication Data

Parrott, John
  Right on cue : an autobiography.
  I. Title
  794.735092
  ISBN 0 86051 778 0

Typeset, printed and bound in Great Britain by Butler & Tanner Ltd, Frome and London.

Contents

		page
1	Kopped at Anfield	7
2	Growing Up	10
3	One Rainy Day	16
4	Leaving School	30
5	Pontin's	43
6	Television Début	52
7	The Turning Point	57
8	A Winner in Europe	64
9	Karen & Me	71
10	Pressure at the Crucible: Hillsborough and After	79
11	A Near Miss	87
12	Back to Basics	91
13	Champion of the World	96
14	Life at the Top	110
15	Player Tales	116

		page
16	Old Contemporaries	126
17	Friends, Rivals & Others	130
18	Pot Black	156
19	Snooker Calendar	161
20	Burn-out	171
21	The Press	175
22	Head to Head	180

1

Kopped at Anfield

On Saturday, 11 May 1991 I spent a rather special afternoon at Anfield, the famous home of Liverpool football club.

I'd been a Liverpool fan ever since I was 10, when my grandfather, a season-ticket holder, began to take me regularly to Anfield. We used to be at the ground by 1 o'clock on Saturday afternoon. The kick-off wouldn't be for another two hours, but we needed to get there early to make sure of claiming our favourite spot behind a wall towards the back of the Kop. Once we had secured our place, Grandad would go and buy me an orange juice and a sausage roll.

At Liverpool I saw some of the greatest football the British game has to offer. These were the great days when Bob Paisley was manager, Graeme Souness was captain, Kenny Dalglish and Ian Rush were playing together up front, and the club was winning everything in sight. (To be honest, I have to admit that I'm just as keen a fan of Everton. You see, my father was an Everton supporter, so I would be taken every other Saturday to Goodison!) When I began to get seriously involved with snooker, I suppose I lost a little bit of my

7

old passion for football, though I still went to matches regularly and later had season tickets for both clubs.

This particular Saturday, however, was something else. For one thing it was my 27th birthday. For another, my manager Phil Miller and Ken Rogers of the *Liverpool Echo* had arranged with Peter Robinson, Liverpool FC's chief executive, for me to go to Anfield to show off the World Championship snooker trophy I had won five days before by beating Jimmy White in the final.

I spent part of that morning visiting a young man called Philip Bragg, who is paralysed from the neck down. A useful snooker player, Philip was mad keen on sports before his injury, which happened in a rugby match when the scrum collapsed on top of him. Just after his accident a couple of years previously, I had played an exhibition at a local club for Philip's benefit. He's a real fighter and this time it was a pleasure to show him the World Championship trophy and pose with him and his family while the cameras clicked away.

At Anfield they had laid on a four-course lunch for Phil and me. Afterwards there was some difficulty in getting seats for us in the directors' box – it was Liverpool's last home game of the season, against Tottenham – but eventually two guests were persuaded to move. Phil sat by two distinguished graduates of the Boot Room, Bob Paisley and Joe Fagan, while on my side were some of the Spurs entourage; I wished them luck in the FA Cup final the following Saturday.

And then it was my moment. As I waited in the players' tunnel, I heard over the loudspeakers the familiar voice of the announcer who has been part of the Anfield pre-match build-up for years: '... We have a very special guest today. He has brought some silverware to Merseyside, and I think you all know who he is....'

There were 36,000 of the best supporters in the world at Anfield that day. As I walked onto the pitch they all seemed to be standing up and cheering. 'Champion!...Champion!...Champion!' echoed around the stadium. And then the Kop broke into 'There's only one Johnny Parrott', as only they can. Merseysiders are proud of their sporting heroes, and are never reluctant to show it. For a scouser like me it was one of the greatest moments of my life.

2

Growing Up

My parents Alan and Eileen were divorced when I was
four, and from then until I was 14 I was brought up by
my uncle George and aunt Freda, who lived in Stanley
Street in the Garston district of Liverpool. My Mum
remarried and moved to Oxford. My Dad, who was a
painter and decorator by trade, remained in the family
home in Ramilies Road, Wavertree, which is six or
seven miles from Stanley Street. He has never remarried, and at the time of the divorce he was employed as
a tyre inspector at Dunlop's, in the Speke district of
the city.

I know very little about my parents' problems and
why they split up. What I do know is that Mum and
Dad now get on famously, which is great. What is even
greater is that Dad, Mum and stepfather Tony Beasley
are the best of friends. They go out shopping and have
dinner together, and Dad thinks the world of Tony. It's
a real pleasure for me to see the three of them getting
on so well with each other.

I will always be grateful to George and Freda (my
mother's sister) for the way they brought me up. They
made sure I had respect, good manners, was always

clean and tidy and did everything properly. If I was out of line I had a good belting. I was treated as if I was one of their own and I had to do as I was told. You hear of people these days who say you shouldn't hit your kids. Well, a good crack around the ear didn't do me any harm. They have a son called Stuart who was like a little brother to me. He is six years younger and I used to keep an eye on him when he was a toddler. Now he is a big strapping lad who is in the hotel business and doing well for himself.

Dad would call some evenings to see me. At other times he would catch the bus home rather than disturb me if I was playing in the park with my friends and enjoying myself.

As I grew up I used to see Mum a couple of times a year. There were problems at one stage when I started to play tournament snooker. She would come to Liverpool without knowing my itinerary and sometimes I wasn't there. Mum would be a little upset, but there was really nothing I could do about it if I was to make my way in the game.

Apart from the times when I have been on television, Mum hasn't seen me play much. Stepfather Tony is a very keen snooker fan, and although he has been able to come to only a few tournaments, he rarely misses any of my matches on TV. He and I are mad about cars; we both own BMWs, read the same motor magazines, and have been to Oulton Park together to watch the car racing. It was Tony who brought Mum and Dad to the Crucible Theatre in May 1991 so that we could all share my greatest-ever achievement in winning the Embassy World Championship.

11

I used to stay with my Dad at weekends. He would pick me up on a Friday evening and take me back to Freda's on Monday morning. This is when I got my sporting outlets – he would take me to the football or for a spot of golf at the local pitch-and-putt course, or things like that.

My first school, at Banks Road in Garston, was very close to my aunt's home; but to get to New Heys Comprehensive, where I went when I was eleven, I had to catch the bus which used to stop at the top of the street. When I moved back with Dad to the Penny Lane area and Ramilies Road, it was still a bus ride to school, only now the journey was in the opposite direction.

I enjoyed school but I had no great sporting interests at New Heys once snooker had taken over my life. I couldn't be bothered playing any other games and was far less active outdoors than I had been at the junior school. Some of my mates thought this was a bit odd, living in a football-mad city and not wanting to play soccer. Snooker then had hardly been heard of in Liverpool. All the kids in the street kicked a football around. They were rather like the kids in Brazil who spend all their spare time playing football on Copacabana beach – except that Merseyside isn't blessed with miles of golden sand. Girls, they never interested me: I didn't have my first kiss until I was 16.

I kept some of the reports from my schooldays. The gist of them hardly changed over the years. 'Would be better served reading a wide range of literature than sport-orientated magazines' was a constant theme – I was always reading about snooker or (occasionally) other games. I liked to read about things I was interested in; it was difficult to concentrate on anything else.

When I was 13 I saw Steve Davis play for the first time at the Albert Hall in Lark Lane, Aigburth. The table he played on had been installed some 10 years earlier, and precious few centuries had been made on it, possibly only six or seven. The middle pockets were desperately tight and the hardest shot on the table was to pot from baulk either the yellow or green off their spots into the centre pockets.

Steve was taking part in a challenge series with Russell Jarmack; their opponents were George Scott and Doug French. Davis had played only three or four shots when Dad leaned towards me and whispered, 'He'll do – he'll be a world champion one day.' Although Dad was never a particularly good player himself, he's always been a shrewd judge of latent talent at the snooker table.

A lot of people have asked me why Dad rarely comes along to watch me play these days – he was a fairly regular spectator in years gone by. The truth is, I've banned him: it's better for both of us this way.

The reason is that just before I was due to play Neal Foulds in the semi-finals of the 1986 UK championship, my Dad had a stroke. (I lost to Neal 9–3 but in a way I was pleased that I managed to win a few frames because I'm very close to my father and it was a very upsetting time for me.)

I first got wind that something wasn't right with him when he returned to our house after doing the washing at a nearby laundrette. I was about to start practising when he told me he wasn't feeling too good and that he had pains in his left side. I'd never known Dad to be sick before, apart from a gallstone complaint he'd had several years earlier. It was unusual for him even to catch a cold. I must admit I didn't know what to make of it all. Fortunately, Phil rang Dad later and sensed straight away that something wasn't right with him as his speech sounded a little slurred. Phil came over to the house, and on seeing Dad he had an idea what was wrong – his wife's father had suffered a stroke only a couple of months earlier. Phil called in the doctor, who decided it was best to get Dad into hospital at once. He stayed there a couple of days while doctors gave him a thorough going over.

One of the first things he had to do when he was allowed home again was to lose weight and take things easy. He was prescribed tablets to help his hypertension. He was a good patient because he was very sensible about it all, even though he had to curb his eating habits. He's a bit like me, he likes his food but doesn't drink much at all.

At the time of this illness we had been at the house for only a little while and Dad, who's a born worrier, was a bit apprehensive about our ability to keep up our repayments on the mortgage. Phil told him firmly to put his mind at rest about this. And although things were pretty tight for a while, I did well at one of the tournaments not long afterwards, which helped to take the pressure off.

If you can be lucky to have a stroke, Dad was because it didn't cripple him in any way and yet it served as a warning to take more care of himself. He is now in the peak of health and to look at him you would hardly think he'd suffered a day's illness in his life.

Anyway, one of the consequences of all this was that I found I was unable to concentrate properly if Dad came to watch me play. Steve Davis and his father Bill are not bothered by this problem; neither are two other father and son teams, Terry and Martin Griffiths and Neal and Geoff Foulds. But it certainly affected me. Dad is inclined to get a bit red in the face when watching me play, and as you can imagine, this didn't do my game any favours at all.

So we agreed it was best for him to stay at home and for me to get on with the job of playing snooker without having any extraneous pressures to contend with. I pointed out to him that he would still be able to watch many of my matches on television, and that in any case the constant travelling from tournament to tournament wouldn't do him any good, never mind the excitement when I was at the table.

Now every time I play he gets a report almost as soon as the last ball has been potted – we always phone him with the result (which in any case he can always check out on Ceefax or Oracle). Mind you, we still have long postmortems on the matches as soon as I get to see him after a major tournament.

Dad is perfectly happy with this arrangement. He is very independent because that's the way circumstances have turned out, and he doesn't like things to interrupt what he wants to do – which most of the time these days is playing crown-green bowls. This is fine by me: the exercise is good for him and he is sure of good company at his bowls club.

3

One Rainy Day

I had my first real look at a full-sized snooker table
when I was about eleven years old. I was with my
father, a friend of his and his young son, and we had
planned to play a game of bowls at the 'Mystery' – a
Wavertree park so-called because nobody knew who it
belonged to. Almost as soon as we arrived it started to
rain. There was no point in trying to play in the wet,
so my Dad suggested we pop along to the nearby Dudley
Institute, where he was a member and where there was
a couple of tables. I didn't know what to expect, but I
was intrigued because Dad had told me about the
Dudley. Here was the chance to see it for myself.

The four of us went in and I was immediately hooked
by the atmosphere and just seeing the balls go into the
pockets: I'd never seen the balls actually go down the
pocket and along the running rail before. It all seemed
so compelling. My eyes were popping out, and when
Dad put our names on the board for a game, I couldn't
wait to play.

Time went slowly but eventually it was our table and
a coin – 10p for 20 minutes – went into the meter. The
lights came on, and after Dad had set up the balls we

16

were ready to play, using a couple of cues from out of the rack.

My friend and his father soon left – they didn't seem interested in snooker. But by the time the first game was over I was smitten by the snooker bug. From that day on, Dad and I made a habit of going to the club on Saturday afternoons whenever possible.

I really shouldn't have been in the club at all because I was under age; but Dad was a minor shareholder so he had a little bit of clout. The Dudley officially opened at 6 o'clock on Saturday evenings. But Dad managed to get hold of a key and had a duplicate made, enabling us to get in when the place was supposed to be closed.

Soon snooker was all I used to think about and I just couldn't get to the table often enough. Dad bought a second-hand cue for me from another member of the club for the princely sum of five bob (25p)! The cue was cut down a bit to suit me, but never had a ferrule put on. (I've kept my first-ever cue and it's still in the rack at home.)

Cues can be quite a problem for kids when they first take up the game. If you stand a cue on its butt, the ferrule should reach to the height of your armpit. But teenagers grow fast, so they frequently need to acquire new cues or splice in extra length at the butt end of an existing one. The trouble is, it's almost impossible to duplicate the exact qualities of a favourite cue: the new or extended one may have identical physical properties – and yet for some reason may not feel quite right. And if you don't have total confidence in your cue, your game will fall apart.

I went through a number of under-size cues before I

was tall enough to have a full-size one. The best of
these was bought after I won the north-west regional
under-16s tournament and so qualified for the quarter-
finals of the national under-16s championship. My Dad
ordered this cue from Stuart Surridge, the cricket-ball
manufacturer. It cost £24 and was a real beauty, 'just
like a wand,' as Dad would say. (It was eventually sold
to a Scotsman for £35.)

We visited a number of specialist shops before paying
£50 for my first full-size cue. It was made of ash and
when I started practising I found it was too whippy. So
we sold it back to the shop for the loss of a fiver.
Eventually I settled for an Adam two-piece maple cue
similar to the ones Dennis Taylor and John Spencer
were using at the time. We bought mine from Cliff
Wilson, who was wheeling and dealing from a chalet
at Pontin's.

Before I played on a full-size table at the Dudley, Dad
had seen an advert for a 6-foot snooker table in a local
newspaper. It was virtually new and he bought it for
£25. The table was installed in the front room of our
house in Ramilies Road, which was only two streets
away from the Dudley.

Dad's transport in those days was an Austin A35 van,
so to get the table from A to B we put it on top of the
roof rack and brought it home that way. I remember
that van very well. It had leather seats, which today
would probably cost a fortune. The van had a mind of its
own, and when you turned the ignition off the engine
continued to chug away for a few seconds. But, if it
liked to keep going, it wasn't always very eager to start
and some mornings we had to use a crank handle. Still,

all in all it served us well and I was sorry when we had to sell it.

We had a nice big front room at Ramilies Road and there was plenty of space for the table. I pestered my Dad to put it up straight away. It had no legs, just six small screw-in sections which you adjusted to make sure the bed was perfectly horizontal after you had placed it on top of an ordinary table. (There was actually enough space in the room to accommodate a full-size table, but the bay window at one end would have made cueing very difficult, so that was out of the question.)

I played a lot of snooker on this table – Dad says it used to keep me out of trouble – but of course it wasn't the same as having a game on a full-size one. Over at the Dudley, Dad started coaching me. He was only a moderate player, but he had thoroughly absorbed the lessons embodied in Joe Davis's books *How I Play Snooker* and *Advanced Snooker*. For a time I wasn't allowed to play a proper game of snooker. As the first step, Dad wanted me to develop a good cue action. The great stylists in snooker may look as if they were born with a cue in their hands, but in fact a good, reliable cue action is the result of years of hard work. Some of Dad's coaching was a bit mechanical and tedious, but there's no doubt that he gave me an essential grounding in basic technique.

Dad and I would go to the Dudley at around 2 o'clock on Saturday afternoon and leave just after the soccer results, some three hours later.

To learn how to achieve a good cue action I had to strike the cue ball up and down the spots, from brown

19

to black and back. Later on, Dad put a red on either side of the black spot. Now I had to send the cue ball over the spots again without touching the two reds. The next step was to add a red on either side of the pink spot, then two more by the blue spot. This is a very good way of learning how to strike the cue ball cleanly in the centre. You will avoid hitting the red balls only if you are able to strike the cue ball without imparting the slightest suspicion of side-spin.

It was about six months before I started making 50-plus breaks quite regularly. This was already better than my Dad, whose highest break was 51 although he had been playing for years. Fifty-odd wasn't a bad break in those days; there weren't many much higher than that being made in local league snooker. I played with the heavy old crystalate balls. My right arm was like Popeye's, you had to hit those balls so hard to get them around the table.

To complicate break building at the top of the table, Dad would put a piece of cloth in the jaws of one of the top pockets. Only the other top pocket was available, and I had to work my way around, potting red, black, red, and so on. Sometimes the blue was the only colour allowed on the table apart from the reds, so often the only way to maintain position after potting one of the reds or the blue was to force the cue ball around the cushions.

We didn't pay any attention to safety play at this stage: all I did was pot balls. But as the coaching became a little more advanced I had to practise potting the blue in such a way as to take the cue ball into and out of baulk without hitting the yellow, green or brown which were on their spots. The benefit of practice like this was clearly demonstrated a few years later when I made a break of 100 at the Cherry Tree in St Helens, Lancs. It was something of a record because I reached my century without once potting the pink or black. (I remember playing Doug French at the Cherry Tree in a challenge match. Doug, who turned professional for the second time in 1991, was the English amateur championship runner-up in 1971; but that night – I think I was 17 at the time – I won 5–1 or 5–2. Doug, always the comedian, remarked to the audience afterwards: 'I think you have seen a future world champion this evening. If you have a few minutes, I'll tell you how I will do it.')

By the age of 13 I would do anything to make sure I could play at the Dudley, so it wasn't long before I was brushing and ironing the two tables there. I was given the key to the equipment cupboard and, believe me, from then on those tables were always spotlessly clean.

I was still going to New Heys Comprehensive school at the time and fitted in the snooker whenever I could. I liked school, and enjoyed my soccer and cricket: in fact, if it rolled I either kicked it or hit it. At my first school, in Banks Road, we had won the Liverpool schools southern area under-11 soccer championship and had drawn 1–1 in the overall final against the northern winners, Broad Square, to share the trophy. I played on the left wing and still have my medal.

Now, on my way home from New Heys, I would pop into the Dudley. Dad would call for me later on his way home from work. In the meantime I did my 'homework' or played in four-handers with some of the more senior members who went in; but they 'barred me out' when the breaks I put together became too big for their standard.

By the age of 14 I was back living with my father. After all, I was old enough to look after myself now, and snooker practice took over my life outside school. Saturday was the big day. I would strap my cue on to the cross bar of my bike and head for the Aigburth People's Hall, where I practised from nine till mid-day. After lunch at home I would go on to the Dudley for another session from one till six. Then I'd dash home for tea, but within an hour I would be back at the Dudley, practising from seven until midnight.

The People's Hall at Aigburth is still going strong. It's a nice little club and was about three miles from where I lived. Juniors were allowed to play from 10 till mid-day on a Saturday morning. That was far too short a time for me, and I used to drive the club's steward crazy by banging on his door at eight o'clock. The trouble was, Friday night was his evening off and he liked to bend his elbow, hoping for a lie-in the next morning. I imagine he must have cursed me long and loud for ruining his beauty sleep.

I occasionally played on Sundays during those early days. I used to borrow Dad's key to the Dudley and play for a good few hours with a friend who lived around the corner. Another good friend from school, Alex Garland, took me to the NUR Club where his father Harry was a member. Alex was quite a good player himself and we often went in for an hour or so on a Monday night before anyone else got there.

My snooker career was to begin in earnest when I

22

started playing in the league. I was still only 14 years of age and didn't have a clue how things would go, but I eagerly looked forward to my very first match.

It was also at this stage that another Liverpool player, George Scott, who was then still an amateur, came into the picture. Dad was looking for someone who was capable of making life tough for me on the green baize, and Scotty was the ideal choice. He was a tremendously tough competitor – he'd won the Merseyside championship no less than 13 times – and at the time his safety play seemed to me like granite. I used to go to his house on Saturdays. My Dad told me he would be a hard man to beat, but at the same time would provide the right kind of opposition. The general feeling was that I didn't know how to win correctly.

After several sessions with Scotty I felt I would never beat him. Dad used to tell me, 'Yes, he'll take some licking. But when you do beat him, you'll know you're improving.'

Well, that's where all my coaching started, with my father. He has never been one to blow his own trumpet and over the years has said little about this. But as far as the basics are concerned, Dad taught me everything.

Since those early days dozens of people have helped me to gain even more knowledge about the game of snooker, though without a shadow of doubt the biggest influences on my career, both on and off the table, have been my father Alan and my manager Phil Miller, who was quite a good player in his day.

At the Dudley the snooker captain, George Gilroy, happened to be a very good friend of my Dad, who has known him for years. He is a local shopkeeper and a

character in his own right. I'd stand in his shop sometimes and watch him at work. His method was rather
like Ronnie Barker's in *Open All Hours* – he had this
unnerving ability to persuade shoppers to spend any
loose change owing to them after making a purchase.

Dad asked George to put me straight into division
one, knowing full well I would have a tough time. The
standard was very high, but I could only benefit from
the experience. I was expected to lose my first matches,
and in fact I went six or seven games without winning.
To his credit, George kept me in the side, and soon
enough I got win number one under my belt.

I remember only too well my very first match. It was
against a chap called John Ball, who I still see now
and again. He always winds me up about it. John
'tonned me' on my league début, winning 100–28, and
in the return match at the Dudley he beat me again.
John has resolutely refused to play me since then. After
all, he argues, how many people have a 100 per cent
victory record against John Parrott?

Because my Dad played in another team, George
Gilroy or another team-mate would pick me up for the
away matches (it was only a hop and skip for me when
we played at home), and I will always be grateful to
them for their help.

The Dudley was not used only for snooker: it was
basically a social club. One of the rooms upstairs was
directly over part of the snooker room and was hired
out once a week or so for spiritualist meetings. One
night me and my mates decided to wind them up while
they were holding a seance. One of the lads stood at
the top of the stairs listening to what was going on at

the seance; another stood at the bottom of the stairs, while I waited in the snooker room. When one of the spiritualists cried out, 'Can you hear me?' I was given the signal – and thumped the ceiling with my cue. Some of the old folk emerged from the seance white faced and trembling like a leaf. They discovered later it was all a joke, but I don't think they know to this day who was banging the cue.

Our snooker room was like nothing I'd seen before or am likely to see again. We had two tables, both made by a small Liverpool company called Bailiffs in about 1906 and renovated some years before my time by Ashcroft's, a local firm. The tables, especially the one used for matches, were in pretty good shape – which is more than you could say for the club premises. The snooker room was furnished, if that's the word, with these antediluvian sofas, whose springs were coming up through the seat and whose frames squeaked and groaned when you moved. There was only one window in the room. You might have thought the club committee would have invested in a cheap blind or pair of curtains to prevent sunlight dazzling the players at the table. Not at the Dudley! Oh no – they painted the whole window – glass and all – with thick black paint. And just in case anyone had the idea of opening the window to let out the fug, they had screwed the casement to the frame.

There was no shortage of fug in the snooker room, especially in winter. There was an ancient gas-fire heater which compensated for its inability to heat the room by producing inordinate quantities of carbon monoxide. On some weekday afternoons the room would be loud with the snores of pensioners who were sitting too close to the fire. I remember on one occasion they had to send for the ambulance because one old party could not be woken.

Opposing teams dreaded coming to the Dudley. I remember one year, when we were in the Bootle League, this team called Walton Trades had to come to the club. They were a top side – they had won the League title for five years and had some very fine players – but we beat then 7–0. Their howls of complaint were loud and long: 'We're going to get this place thrown out of the League. How the hell can we play when there's a bucket hanging over the table?'

Ah, yes, the bucket! Above the black spot end of the match table, a timber beam stretched from one side of the room to the other. Someone had nicked the lead flashing from the section of roof immediately above the beam and the club committee had not seen fit to have it properly repaired. The result was that when it rained, the roof leaked and water dripped from the beam. So a bucket was hung from the beam to catch the water. On rainy match nights the religious hush of the snooker room would be broken by the tinkle, tinkle, tinkle of water dripping into the bucket.

One memorable evening the bucket fell off its hook and some of its contents saturated the black spot end of the table. The visiting team were unable to come back another night. So we all agreed to carry on. During one frame, one of their players tried to roll the black along the top cushion. The ball never reached the pocket, squelching to a halt scarcely halfway to its destination.

The bucket is still a talking point. A friend of mine,

Steve Jones, got married recently, and some of his mates who had played with him at the Dudley presented him with an almost identical bucket as a special wedding present. It brought the house down at the reception.

Eventually my Dad got so embarrassed about the state of the snooker room that he went round one afternoon and painted everything in it that needed painting. The club secretary, true to the spirit of generosity prevailing among the committee members, not only thanked him but presented him with a bottle of lemonade – absolutely free.

Just before I finished playing league snooker at the Dudley I made a total clearance of 129. It was the first century break ever made in a one-frame league match on Merseyside. It was also my first competitive match century.

The Dudley billiards team were playing on the other table, but my century failed to impress these more senior members. As a huge roar greeted the end of my clearance, their captain came over to complain about the cheering. The snooker players were a bit flabbergasted by this behaviour and John Young, a member of the visiting snooker team, gave him the verbals. I have a memento of that break in the form of a certificate signed by the late Bill Cottier, then the chairman of the Billiards & Snooker Control Council. It's one of my most treasured possessions because it was the last one signed by Bill, who died before I actually received it.

In spite of everything, there was a great atmosphere at the Dudley. The lads took the mickey out of the place – you had to. It was said that if you played at the

Dudley you developed a good cue action and a great sense of humour.

In fact, the atmosphere at most of the local clubs was good, and one or two had their own peculiarities. There was one club where you had to use a shortened cue if you got stuck by a protruding section of wall. At another some woman, who was more houseproud than clever, thought she had done us all a favour one day by waxing the floor. Of course we couldn't stand properly, it was so slippery, and I think more lads left that club with hernias than you could shake a stick at. If you bent over for a shot your feet would go from under you; it was impossible to stand up.

I also remember my first ever visit to the Dingle club. There were pictures of naked women on the walls, and as at that time the subject was unfamiliar to me, the sight didn't do my game much of a favour. Then there was the Thingwall club in Thingwall Lane. That place was in a different league: it was just a shed with two tables. Everything was sold on trust. If you wanted a can of coke (they didn't have beer) you just took one and left the money in a bag. It was also twopence in the meter. We played for hours there. One day a bloke barred me from going to this club. I was 17 and had already played in the Northern final of the English championship, but he said I couldn't go in until I was 18. I met him again last year and he asked me for a photograph. I told him where to put it.

Every year the Dudley was among the top teams in the league and attracted some of the best players in the area, including Ian Brumby, who is now a professional. My future manager Phil Miller also joined.

One Rainy Day

I stopped playing league snooker when I was about 17 because to spend an evening just to play one frame and then mark another was wasting valuable time. I needed all the hours I could get to practise and compete in the extensive programme of competitions for which Phil was entering me. But I had enjoyed my league snooker and was sorry to have to let it go.

After turning professional, and right up until the club was sold in 1988, I would go back to the Dudley whenever I could to see my friends there. The place has recently been refurbished and it's now used solely for functions. Its snooker days are over.

4
Leaving School

I left school when I was 17 with no other thought than
making a career out of snooker. It had never seriously
crossed my mind to do anything else. The teachers at
New Heys thought this was rather foolish, and I can
see their point. One of them, John Walsh, considered I
would do better if I stayed on at school, and he suggested I started playing football again. But by now I
preferred to watch – I absolutely hated playing. John
was the PE instructor and he refused to allow my
suggested arrangement by which I would practise my
snooker instead of doing PE. (I had a letter from him
after winning the World Championship in which he
wrote 'How wrong can you be?' He's a smashing bloke,
and I have been back to the school a few times to see
the kids in his class.)

My parents had opposing views about my leaving
school. I think Dad, a great jazz fan, had had visions
when I was a lot younger of John Parrott becoming a
top trombonist; but he realized soon enough that I
could play far better with a cue in my hand than I ever
would with a 'bone', and he was in complete agreement
with my plans. Mum, on the other hand, was mortified.

She thought my education should come first. But living in Oxford with my stepfather she didn't really know what was going on. In any case it would not have impressed her if she had been told I might become English amateur champion or anything like that.

I left school with O-levels in English, English literature, geography, biology, history and maths. I went on to study A-levels in geography, history, English language and English literature, though after a while I gave up the geography; three subjects were enough, and English Lit. was the one I enjoyed most. I liked my Shakespeare and Dickens, and I had a great teacher, Ken Othen, who later was to come and watch me play in the Lada Classic at Warrington, the event in which I made my television début. Ken (or 'Sir', as I used to call him) was a teacher I thoroughly respected, and at Warrington he wished me all the best for the future.

I studied A-levels only for a year because snooker was now the biggest thing in my life. I realized it was more important to me than looking out of the window on a Wednesday afternoon during a history class. The whole idea of school was boring me stiff by now. It was time to go.

Friends have asked me if it even crossed my mind to take up some form of steady employment when I left school. I can only say that one day, for a split second, I may have thought of being a policeman or a fireman. I didn't have any aspiration to be a rock star or astronaut. I just couldn't envisage doing anything other than play snooker for a living. While some kids in the class would be reading *Striker* or *Shoot* or some other soccer magazine, I'd have my head buried in *Cue World* or *Snooker Scene*.

The first snooker club to open in Liverpool was the Golden Leisure, and even before leaving school I was offered free practice there. I became very friendly with everyone, and to repay the practice facility I looked after the tables, all eighteen of them. This was a fantastic club, the atmosphere was superb and table three, the match table, was a cracker. I had some great matches on it. I would get to the club between nine and ten in the morning, clean and iron the tables, and play with a friend, Jimmy Jenkins, who worked behind the bar and collected up the glasses. We used to have a daily 'cheeseburger challenge'. I would give him a start (say 35 a frame) and we would play a set number of frames. Whoever lost would have to buy the food from the burger bar on the corner. I think I lost once or twice, but it was a good incentive to keep me playing.

There were some rum goings on at another club, called the City Road. Phil used to go there and told me that much of the fun and games concerned a Chinese seaman called Johnny Lin, who was half Chinese and half English. He liked to gamble, so when he came home on shore leave with his pockets full of money he would play anyone for anything. Everyone would queue up to take him on. If you had no money, it didn't matter: he would play you for your shirt, his own usually being a real technicolor specimen he had bought on his last voyage to Honolulu or other places with romantic names.

Johnny was a real gambler. He once played Phil for 10 bob. That was all the money Phil had with him, but by the end of the evening he had won £50. Johnny Lin loved snooker and would play even if he got little out of it; at various times he lost his bike, his watch, his ties – even a pair of shoes he had bought in New York.

The most extraordinary tale I heard about Johnny Lin was when he went into the City Road just before Christmas with a live turkey under his arm. He was skint but got someone to play him for the festive bird, which he tied to the leg of the snooker table with a piece of string. He lost – and we always wondered what his family had to eat for Christmas that year. Johnny could go through hundreds of pounds when he was on shore leave. He would even have side bets with the people standing around the table – a crowd always gathered to watch him play.

I've been in the Golden Leisure when it was full of Chinese. The club closed only for four hours for cleaning, staying open from around 11am until 7am. At night it would be heaving with them. They all loved to gamble, and the silliest thing I ever did was to play well in front of them. I could have earned a fortune if I had been crafty and fiddled around like a novice. They were having £100 a frame and couldn't play the game.

I can mention it now because the Golden Leisure has long gone, but there was such a colourful crowd in there that hardly a day went by when someone didn't come in to flog a hookey video, television or anything they could get their hands on. Nothing unusual about videos, you might say – except that this happened long before they were on sale in the shops in this country. Never mind falling off the back of a lorry – these must have jumped off the deck of a ship.

One day all the players in the team were talking about changing their cues, for one reason or another. All of a sudden a whole batch of the things 'found' their way into the club. They were top-of-the-range cues and worth about £75 each – a lot of money in the early 1980s.

I was still playing at the Dudley when Phil and I got together after I had lost to Ian Williamson at the Commonwealth Club, Blackpool, in the 1980 Northern finals of the English championship. A whole chara full of fans from the Dudley came to support me, and on the way back I couldn't understand how I came to lose. I had been 4–1 ahead in a best of 15 frames match. Phil had travelled on the coach to watch the match. He had joined the Dudley only about six months earlier. When I asked him why he thought I had been beaten he explained it in one word: experience. He said that the only way I would learn how to win was to start playing in tournaments up and down the country.

I still hadn't quite reached my sixteenth birthday when I went with Phil, who by now was my manager, to play my first match under his wing. It was at Mobberley in Cheshire, and Dave Williams of Stoke beat me 3–2. I was like a duck out of water, completely inexperienced. It certainly wasn't plain sailing in those days and I remember another occasion when Phil took me in his geriatric Ford Escort to a junior snooker tournament at a golf club near Swindon. That's about an eight-hour round journey, and we left at 4am so as to arrive in plenty of time for a 9 o'clock start. Between Knutsford and Keele the car broke down. It was pouring with rain and Phil had to get out of the car and try and get the thing going again. It burst into life after a 20-minute delay. By now Phil was soaked through by the spray from passing lorries, and I couldn't stop laughing at his appearance – he looked worse than Catweasel. I couldn't have helped him because I didn't know anything about car engines (I know little more even now). I wasn't old enough to drive, so why should I get out of the car and get wet?

We eventually arrived at the tournament in time for me to make a prompt start to my match at 9 o'clock. Half an hour later we were ready for the journey back to Liverpool. I'd lost 2–0 in short order. There wasn't even a radio in the car to relieve the misery and boredom of the drive home. It's at times like this that you question the wisdom of what you are trying to achieve. But it's surprising how attitudes change after a good night's sleep and an even better practice session.

During the next eighteen months Phil entered me in everything possible. I played in over 300 matches and started to get into the habit of winning. The last season before I turned professional was my best, and by then I had a number of titles under my belt.

My father had chauffeured me to the junior matches until Phil took over. Occasionally he had had to take time off from work, and this cost him a fair amount of money. Dad was with me when I lost in the 1979 final of the British Under-16 championship to Tony Pyle of Exeter. He was one of Jack Karnhem's pupils and I lost 3–2 on the black. That was a disappointment because at the time I thought I was a better player. On the day, though, Tony's extra experience saw him through, and only my ability got me to 2–2.

Already the seeds had been sown for that 'brides-maid' tag that some journalists would later hang on me. It would haunt me for quite a few years, and continued in the 1980 British Under-16 championship final. This time Terry Whitthread beat me – though this was only to be expected because he was light-years ahead of me and had been playing the game since he was about 10. Terry was the big buzz from London and at 15 was an exceptionally good player. He was beating everybody and I lost 3–1. No grumbles.

Neal Foulds was in the other corner for the 1982 British Under-19 final. I remember potting the blue in the fourth frame. That should have given me a 3–1 victory – but I went in-off, and Neal went on to win that frame and the decider. This was another big disappointment. I had played well enough to win the match, but it wasn't to be. Once the score had gone to 2–2, Neal was always favourite to win.

The English championship remained the one amateur title I wanted to win most of all, and after losing 8–6 to Malcolm Bradley in the 1982 Northern final I was determined to have one more crack at it (and hopefully also gain selection for England in the home internationals) before applying for professional status.

During the next 12 months I won all my four matches for England. But I could do no better than finish runner-up to Tony Jones in the 1983 English final – the biggest disappointment of my amateur career. I had waited so patiently for another chance to win the championship, reaching the all-England play-off following an 8–4 victory over Steve Meakin in the Northern area final. Tony came through from the Southern area finals. He defeated Neal Foulds 8–6 and the final was decided over 25 frames at Stantonbury Leisure Centre, Milton Keynes.

What happened? Well, to start with I picked up the worst bout of 'flu I have ever had in my life. I've never known anything like it. I was in bed for five days, and Phil had to get me out of my sick bed to play in the final. I didn't feel like playing, but from 5–1 down I managed to get to 8–8 and then 9–9 with a break of 78, the highest of the final. Tony, who was a little wiser in the head than I was, then won the next four frames and that was it. I was a runner-up again.

Phil and I agreed I shouldn't mention anything about being ill. Tony had played well to win and we didn't want to take anything away from him. I was pleased with my own performance but so disappointed I had lost, even though on form Tony was a bit ahead of me and Neal. I considered the three of us to be the best amateurs in the country at the time.

During that last season I had won 14 out of 18 competitions, which was worth over £10,000 to me, quite a bit of money in those days. The titles included the Liverpool Under-21, the Merseyside championship, Pontin's, the Stockton Pro-am, and the Silver Cue at the Astra Club in Birmingham. It was some consolation, but I left Milton Keynes feeling dejected; after all, I had held back to become English champion and it hadn't worked out.

My application to turn professional went into the post straight after the English final, and the board of the World Professional Billiards & Snooker Association soon replied to confirm that I had been accepted.

Phil Miller seems to me the ideal manager. He is a very loyal man and I'm a very loyal player. There is no way I would ever want to change our business relationship. He does well out of my snooker these days, of course, but there were times when he had to dig deep into his own pocket, and that must have been very hard for him bearing in mind that he had a family to keep and a mortgage to pay.

Our business relationship has operated in a professional manner from day one. A contract was signed with the approval of my father, and that same contract remains in force today. Nothing has been added or changed. We now have our own company as well, Six Colours Promotions. Phil does everything for me on the organizational and practical side, and I can rely on him doing it right.

Over the years we have become very close friends. I'm always more than welcome at his home in Allerton, where he lives with his wife Jean, son Duncan and daughter Janette. In our early years together I used to love going round there on a Saturday evening. Phil would have a large selection of Chinese dishes which he had ordered from a local restaurant and we'd all enjoy a really good nosh.

It was through the Dudley that Dad and myself got to know Phil. He used to be in textiles, but he gave up that job during my third year as a professional, when it had become clear that it was a full-time job organizing my career.

I have had approaches to move elsewhere – notably from Barry Hearn and Ian Doyle – but I never wanted to be part of a set-up of seven or eight players. Hearn and Doyle are snooker's 'big two' and are inclined to be more outspoken, more vociferous than we are. Phil and I prefer the softly, softly approach and go about things in our own way.

When I joined Howard Kruger's Framework, he acted only as an agent. It was the same during my association with Ian Doyle's Scottish-based Cue-Masters set-up. I went to Howard at a time when I was going through an indifferent patch. Phil and I agreed that an agent might help to keep me out of the limelight while I got my game together again. In this respect the move paid off, because that season I worked my way into the top 16 for the first time, taking over the No. 13 spot.

Howard had quite a few top players at that time, including Joe Johnson, Dean Reynolds, Tony Knowles, Alex Higgins, Martin Clark and, for a month at the outset, Jimmy White. But things didn't really work out happily for me at Framework, and after a year I left.

One of the highlights of that period was a trip to China just before the 1988 World Championship. It was one of the nicest trips I have ever been on and Phil, myself and the other players had a great time. It was a sort of in-house tournament for Framework players, held in the Chinese capital, Beijing, and in the final I beat Martin Clark 5–1. We were told that the estimated television audience was over 200 million, though only about 800, who paid about 10p each, came to watch in person.

After Framework I joined CueMasters, and thought the set-up was ideal, as Ian Doyle already had Stephen Hendry, Mike Hallett and Darren Morgan on his books. Three of us were in the top six in the world ranking list: I was at No. 2, Stephen at 3, and Mike at 6. The reason the set-up looked ideal was simply that there was a good core group of four players. But soon more players were signed, and by the time I left the team strength was up to seven.

Apart from the fact that I now felt there were too many players at CueMasters there was a conflict of personalities between Phil and Ian Doyle. They never really hit it off and this sometimes led to a breakdown in communications. On one occasion Phil and I were on the way to a tournament at Trentham Gardens. We pulled in to a petrol station and, as Phil replenished the tank, I went and bought a newspaper and read that CueMasters had signed Nigel Bond. Neither Phil nor myself had heard anything about this from Doyle – yet I was playing Nigel in the quarter-finals that very day!

When we parted company Ian Doyle referred in a statement to an 'unworkable relationship' with Phil, claiming that he found it difficult to promote me in the best possible manner. The fact is, however, that I was beginning to feel overshadowed, and that the ideas and projects that Doyle was coming up with just weren't right for me. Phil is paid to make the final decisions on my career, and I have never had any reason to question his judgement. Even when I was a 15-year-old Phil discussed everything with me and all our decisions were made after thoroughly going through the pros and cons together. Phil has the experience of life and business; I have it in the job I do best, which is playing snooker. I have said in the past and I still maintain that if you are treated as second best you will be inclined to perform as such – and that's just not for me.

Before I became involved with CueMasters there were rumours on the circuit that feelers had been put out for me to join Barry Hearn's Matchroom empire. In fact, I was approached three times. The first time I said 'no' because Barry wanted sole management and Phil would have been left out of things. On the second occasion I was initially in favour. But after talking it over with Phil we decided against it because I had not yet won a major tournament and so was not in the best position to dictate my terms.

Phil and I have always got on well with Hearn. Whenever he had anything to say or do concerning us, he always took the honourable approach by going to Phil and discussing it with him first. The ill-fated StormSeal 1990 UK championship provides a good example of what I mean about Barry. StormSeal went into liquidation shortly after the completion of the championship, and that meant a number of players did not receive their prize money when they should have done. Barry, as the tournament promoter, became liable to settle any outstanding debts. He approached Phil to explain the situation, and Phil told him not to worry: 'Pay us when you can'. Barry promised he would settle up out of his own pocket as soon as he could; and while in my own case it took him seven months, he duly handed over a cheque for £39,000 when I was at Brentwood for the last day of the 1991 Matchroom League fixtures. This was made up of £30,000 for reach-

41

ing the semi-finals and £9000 for the highest break. Phil and I had never doubted for one moment that Barry would fulfil his obligations.

Barry is no saint; everyone is aware that he can be ruthless. But he and the Matchroom stable have done a great deal for the game of snooker in Britain and have opened a lot of lucrative markets by taking the game to other countries. On the other hand, having had experience of belonging to the big stables, I am more than ever convinced that a player is better off either on his own or in a stable with no more than four players. I can't see how one man can personally manage seven or eight players at once. He can't keep them *all* happy, and there's an ever-present potential for discontent among the lesser stars in the stable.

5

Pontin's

I have happy memories of Pontin's and the North Wales holiday camp at Prestatyn, where hundreds of snooker players head for in May every year. Over the years I was fortunate enough to achieve probably the best record of any player who has taken part in the Pontin's annual spring festival: I won the Junior, the Open – as both an amateur and a professional – and the Professional Tournament, and no-one else has done that. (Only one other player, Steve Davis, has won the Open during his amateur and professional careers, but he never won the Junior.)

I first went to Pontin's when I was 13 years of age. My Dad took me; he was an avid watcher of snooker and thought that the May festival would be a good opportunity to test me out against the younger players.

At Prestatyn there were usually six specially installed match tables in the ballroom area downstairs and a further 24 club tables in the snooker room on the top floor of the main complex. One table everyone dreaded playing on was No.7, which was upstairs and right at the back. The cloth on it was thicker than my

43

carpet at home. It was a terror – you had to batter the cue ball everywhere.

I didn't win anything on that first trip to Pontin's in 1977, but two years later I lost 3–1 in the Junior final to Dave Gilbert, who was to turn professional in 1985. I eventually won the Junior in 1981, beating a lad called Don Tate 3–1. (I don't think he plays the game any more; I certainly haven't heard anything about him for a long time.)

Twelve months later I went back to Pontin's and won the big one, the Open, to become the youngest ever holder of the title. That was the first major victory of my career – and to achieve it I had to beat Ray Reardon in the final.

Ray and the other seven invited professionals – Steve Davis, Terry Griffiths, Doug Mountjoy, Willie Thorne, Dennis Taylor, Alex Higgins and John Virgo – were exempt until the event reached the last 32, which meant that from a record entry of over 1056 amateurs, only 24 would go into the draw for the final stages.

I received 25 points a frame but it was still a great feeling to beat the six times world champion 7–4. Ray had defeated Steve Davis off levels 4–0 in the quarter-finals. On my way to the final I had beaten Joe O'Boye (4–0), Alex Sutherland (4–1), Tom Bell (4–1), and Welshman Ivor Tilley 4–3. (I won the last after potting the final blue, pink and black, much to the chagrin of Ivor's many supporters.)

Oddly enough I had practised with Ivor a day or two earlier at a club in Rhyl. I had gone there for a few frames and he came up to me and asked for a game. I had no idea who he was then, so you can imagine our surprise when we discovered we were to be opponents in the semi-finals at Prestatyn.

That year the largest crowd ever assembled for a Pontin's final packed the holiday camp's ballroom. Every available seat was taken as around 2500 spectators waited for the action to start. Many had been there for over two hours. Although admission was free, these were dedicated snooker fans.

Because of the large number of players and their families booked into Pontin's that year, some of the players were allowed to stay in off-camp accommodation – something unheard of before or since. You had to be on site to play, and there have been several instances over the years where players were thrown out of the tournament when it was discovered they were staying at boarding houses in Prestatyn or Rhyl.

When I won the Open for the second time in 1986, I had been a professional for three years. But 12 months earlier I reached the final for the second time, only to lose 7–6 to Jim Chambers, who comes from Walsall. Jim (who has since turned professional) received 25 points a frame and fully deserved his triumph, which climaxed when he potted the pink in the final frame to round off a great match.

There were not quite so many entries in 1986 – just under 800 – but as an invited professional I was again conceding 25 points a frame. My first two victims were Ian Brumby (4–2) and Gary Keeble (4–3). Ian, as I've mentioned already, was once a member of the Dudley Institute; he's one of my best friends and I felt terrible playing him. I then had to play Ray Reardon again for a place in the semi-finals, and off levels I won 4–1.

Ron Jones of Merthyr, another Pontin's regular, was my semi-final opponent. He had beaten John Spencer 4–0 in the quarters so I couldn't afford to take any chances against him. Breaks of 86 and 67 helped me to win 4–1.

The other finalist was Tony Putnam, an amateur who hails from Steve Davis territory in Romford. What a tough match the final proved to be. I led 3–1, 4–2, 5–3 and 6–4, only for Tony to fight back bravely and level the scores after 12 frames. But I kept him at bay in the decider, and with a break of 101 went on to win 7–6. That break would have been the highest of the tournament had I not missed a brown after the last red. So Willie Thorne's 121 took the £500 high-break prize. For winning, I received £2500.

I went back a couple of years later to capture the Professional title, this time beating Stephen Hendry 6–3 in the semi and Mike Hallett 9–1 in the final to complete the grand slam of Pontin's victories. Walter Rowley, the man behind snooker at Pontin's, was among the first to congratulate me. I thanked him and said I was going to have a sex change and would shave my legs as I was thinking of entering the women's event next year in the hope of completing the full set of camp medals.

There was always a special atmosphere at Pontin's. It was a noisy place, full of youngsters and holidaymakers. We were all out for a good time, though this never seriously affected the quality of the snooker. Pontin's was also blessed with some lovable characters, notably Sid Lane, Charlie Hemburrow, Harry Findlay, Ron Gross and Doug French.

Sid, a Merseysider, was a rear gunner in World War
Two. He flew 46 missions, although the maximum
allowed was supposed to be 29. He is a former winner
of the Veterans' tournament, and at one time Phil
worked for him in the textile industry.

Now, Sid doesn't often make a century break. In fact,
when he went to Pontin's in 1982 he had not compiled
a ton since 1939! By the end of that year's festival,
however, Sid had bridged the 43-year gap by notching
another century and on an upstairs table as well. The
more superstitious don't want to see any more 100
breaks from him: World War Two followed the first,
the Falklands War the second. What's he got in store
for us next time?

Sid and Charlie Hemburrow often ran a book on the
Pontin's Open. They weren't the only ones, mind you:
there could be up to half a dozen 'bookies' on site, and
they often ended up betting with each other as one
offered a better price than the rest about a particular
player. Sid won't forget 1980 in a hurry – his friends
won't let him. As he arrived on the camp at Prestatyn
everyone seemed to be pestering him with the same
question: 'What price Jimmy White, Sid?' Sid played it
cagily. He didn't want to take bets on Jimmy, and for
that reason he didn't come up with a price. That turned
out to be a bad idea – Jimmy was beaten in the first
round, and Sid hadn't taken a single bet on him. Had
Sid offered a price, he would have made a real killing;
instead he didn't win a penny, and he's never been
allowed to forget it. Ever since then, 'What price Jimmy
White, Sid?' has been a familiar greeting wherever he
goes.

When I won the 1986 Open, Sid and Charlie had me chalked up as the 5–4 favourite by the time the event reached the semi-final stages. At this point Harry Findlay arrived on the scene. I've got to know Harry quite well since then, but when he came to Pontin's that year no one had the slightest idea who he was or what he did.

Harry is a big man who you wouldn't want to pick a quarrel with, but as he listened intently to the conversation around the Dragonara Bar, the regular watering hole for the Pontin's gamblers, he offered 5–2 about a Parrott victory. Everyone was astonished. They couldn't believe it, and at first thought Harry was trying to wind them up. But he was serious; and Phil borrowed a couple of hundred pounds from Sid and took him at his word: he simply couldn't resist those generous odds. Thereafter, until the Open final was over, Harry was shadowed everywhere he went. Quite a few punters had gone in at 5–2 and, since Harry's was a new face at Pontin's, they were just making sure he had no plans to do a runner with their money.

After the final Harry paid out straight away. When he went to collect his 'monkey', Phil said to him: 'You must have been mad to lay that price.' Harry laughed: 'Why? I was only pawning a bet. I had a grand on John at 100–8 before the tournament started.' Harry is now a familiar figure at most snooker and other sporting events like golf, cricket, rugby, horse and greyhound racing. You name it, he bets on it.

Harry was the owner of a very useful greyhound bitch called Chicita Banana. He bought her in Ireland for about £5000. He brought her over, telling everybody how good she looked and that she was going to be a great dog. Well, the first time she ran, she came out of the traps, sat down and proceeded to unload a great dollop – right in the middle of the track! Harry and the trainer walked over to where she was sitting with a mischievous grin on her face (if a dog can ever have one), calling her all the names under the sun.

Harry of course was pilloried by all his mates, who had backed her heavily. The trainer got to work on her, and eventually she was ready to run again. She ran her second race and won at 20–1. Neither Harry nor his friends had a penny on her in case she succumbed again to a call of nature. The following week she ran again and won at 4–1. Harry slowly began to believe that he really might have a decent racer on his hands.

He wasn't wrong. Chicita Banana went on to win over 20 races, and what's more broke the track record at Wembley held by the immortal Ballyregan Bob. And Harry used to buy everybody in the 'fan club' one of those inflatable bananas, which would be blown up before the dog came out.

Harry's a tremendous character, brilliant. In one of the years I played consistently well, he backed me and won over six figures on my performances over the year. At the time I'd no idea I was earning him money! But later, as a wedding present, he treated Karen and me to a trip on the Orient Express to Venice. He just came up to me and said: 'Here you are, John, that's for you.' There was an envelope, and when I opened it I couldn't believe my eyes.

Harry still insists that it's because of me that he met

his girlfriend. Apparently if I hadn't won a certain match at Sheffield he would have gone home. He had a bet on me each way, and soon after he met his girlfriend who was working as a waitress in the hotel. It's only a few months ago that they had their first baby. He's a great lad, somebody I genuinely like, and one of the real characters on the snooker circuit.

Ron Gross has been another Pontin's regular. He often ran a book on the big tournament there and his booming voice increased in volume the more he drank – and he was very good at doing that. Three times winner of the English amateur championship, Ron is the owner of a snooker hall in London, and his favourite saying has always been, 'Come and play me at my club and I will introduce you to the bottom cushion.' Years ago Ron had Jimmy White, Tony Meo, Tony Jones and Neal Foulds under his wing. One night when he couldn't get a drink after time at the bar at one venue, he bellowed: 'My boys won't play here again unless someone serves me.' At that time Ron's 'boys' had long since left him to join other management teams; but they were at the venue that night and his threat did the trick – much to the amusement of those of us who were watching.

Doug French is another Pontin's regular. I've known him for a good few years because he is a local player who has won the Merseyside championship a few times. I've also known him to change his cue three times in one match. He gets some funny old ideas about snooker. Once he had an array of tips, some of which were wafer thin while others were over-thick. I once saw him play with two tips, one glued on top of the other.

One year at Pontin's I glanced across at his chalet

and saw smoke belching out of the open door. It looked like someone was trying to send a smoke signal. A closer investigation revealed Frenchie holding a frying pan which had no bottom; it had burnt away. He had turned the electric stove on, placed the frying pan on the plate and forgotten all about it. When he cracked an egg and dropped it in, the pan just disintegrated in a cloud of smoke. Deciding that the egg was now unworthy of him, Frenchie nonchalantly tossed it out of the door.

Although a no-hoper in the kitchen, Frenchie could be hot stuff at the snooker table; he was a very good potter and a very forceful player. Every year for about six or seven years they used to give you Pontinental holiday vouchers if you got to the last 32. Frenchie was so successful that every year he and his wife would have holidays abroad virtually for free. Later on, though, Pontin's awarded only vouchers that could be used in the UK.

6

Television Début

I could hardly have picked a more dramatic start to my professional career than facing – and beating – Alex Higgins on my television début. This was in the last 16 of the Lada Classic at the Spectrum Arena, Warrington, in January 1984. This was a superb venue just up the road from home, but unfortunately it's no longer used for snooker. To qualify for the television stages I had beaten Doug Mountjoy 5–4 at the Spectrum the previous month. I'd had to win the last two frames to do so and I remember making a timely clearance of 38 in the eighth game before winning the decider.

Now came the inimitable Mr Higgins, who a few weeks earlier had defeated Steve Davis 16–15 in the pulsating final of the UK championship after losing the first seven frames.

Our first professional confrontation was only over nine frames and by the interval I was leading 4–0, just one frame short of the winning post. It was an incredible start, and although Alex won the next two frames I went on to win 5–2. I still have the video of this match. I occasionally watch it – if only to have a laugh at the way I used to dress and my terrible hair cut. My shirt kept coming out of the back of my trousers; it looked hilarious, rather like Hickey the Firebobby in the old comics.

The atmosphere in the Spectrum had been brilliant. More than 2500 spectators watched the match, which is nearly three times the number who saw each session of my World Championship triumph. The place seemed full of Liverpudlians. They loved it – and Alex took the defeat very well indeed. He came up to me after the match and gave me some useful advice on my game. Not many players would do that.

Tony Knowles was my next victim. He had been on television saying, as only he can, 'I will tame this youngster, I'll teach him what snooker is all about.' I beat him 5–1, an unbelievable performance in front of another 2000-plus crowd.

For the semi-final against Steve Davis the atmosphere was electric. I had never experienced anything like it before. And remember – this was my first game against a player I had long idolized. We shared the first four frames, but I won the fifth on the black with a clearance of 41 to lead 3–2. It was then Steve's turn to show the way. He had a break of 60 in frame six and took the colours to lead 4–3, while I knocked in a 42 to square the match. In the decider I tried a plant into a centre pocket which didn't come off, and Steve went to the table to make a match-winning break of 71.

Having experienced the heady atmosphere of this tournament, I wanted to enjoy it again as soon as possible. The Embassy World Championship gave me the opportunity. I dropped only three frames in the three qualifying rounds at Redwood Lodge, Bristol, and in the last of those defeated the 1978 runner-up, Perrie Mans of South Africa, 10–0. I was gutted for him because he was such a gracious loser and also a very nice, modest man. (If my memory is right, Perrie called it a day the following season, which was a pity because the game has missed a player of his stature, one of the great potters of his time.)

My first opponent at the Crucible in Sheffield was Tony Knowles, who in 1982 had caused an almighty upset by defeating Davis, the holder, 10–1 in the same round. I beat Tony 10–7, then lost 13–11 to Dennis Taylor in a quarter-final match I thoroughly enjoyed.

It was strange the first time I stepped into the arena at the Crucible. The place had an atmosphere like nothing I had ever experienced. The first thing that hits you is having to walk down those steps from the back of the stage. They look horribly steep and you are frightened of falling over.

The 1984 Embassy World Championship marked the end of my first season as a professional. I had learned a great deal already, but there was still a long, long way to go if I was to reach the top of my profession. I was pretty pleased with my progress, though. I was up to No.20 on the world ranking list, and very few players have reached as high as that by the end of their first season.

Three more seasons were to pass before I was able to squeeze into the top 16 at No.13, I reached No.2 in 1989–90, dropped to third in 1990–91 and fourth in 1991–92. One player I'm delighted to see back in the top 16 is Tony Knowles. He's one of my favourite players on the professional circuit, but he's struggled a bit in recent years. Tony is one player who might have something to say to you during a match, but he never does anything with any malice. If we go anywhere on tour, I like to sit next to him on the plane. He can begin a story at Gatwick and by the time you get to Dubai seven hours later he still won't have finished.

I recall playing Tony in 1982 in a pro-am at Stockton, which was a very big event in those days. The club where we played had one of those Starlight tables. Phil made sure, as always, that I arrived early enough for a practice session, and I found that the right-hand side of this particular table tilted fractionally one way.

This meant that with a red anywhere near the cushion on the 'down' side of the table, you had only to aim it in the direction of the top pocket and it *had* to go in. So I was playing position in every match to leave myself on that side of the table. The night I beat Knowlesy I must have potted about seven or eight of these screamers along this one cushion.

Knowlesy wasn't enjoying it at all. He would get out of his chair when it looked for a moment or two as if I had missed. Then, just before the pocket, the ball would almost do a U turn and drop in. Tony's face was a picture.

Phil and I were booked into a local hotel between the semi-finals and final, which were played on successive days. At least we thought it was a hotel, but it turned out to be no more than a boarding house full of navvies from a local building site. We arrived too late for a bite to eat and the kitchen was closed even for a cup of tea, so Phil nipped out and bought a couple of Chinese takeaways and two cans of coke, which we had in the bedroom. Next morning we got up too late for breakfast, but the landlady took pity on us and cooked a lovely meal to send us on our way. It must have inspired me: that evening I won the pro-am, beating John Virgo 4–3.

I also played Tony at the Huddersfield Sports Centre in February 1986 in an exhibition staged by the local Pendragon Round Table. After six frames I was leading 5–1. Three frames later I had finished up the match with successive breaks of 101, 133 and 136. After the 101, I broke off in the next frame and, in opening up the reds, fluked one – and cleared the table. Tony broke off in the last frame and I went back to the table to clear up again. So I had scored 370 on three successive visits to the table, while he had had only one shot – which is possibly some sort of record.

As a tailpiece to the exhibition Tony had been due to attack the world record for the machine-gun shot, which stood at 10. After my 370 points he decided against it. 'How can I follow that?' he asked.

7

The Turning Point

The turning point in my professional career came at the 1987 British Open. I was beaten 5–1 by Warren King in the third round and never made a single break of over 30. It was pathetic.

I returned home and went for a long walk in Calderstones Park. I wanted to be on my own while I pondered the future and what to do about it. I was thoroughly disillusioned with my game. I seriously considered quitting snooker and going out to look for another job. I was only 23 but I was crippled by failure. Both technically and psychologically my game had hit rock bottom. I knew that if I continued playing I would have to force myself to become mentally much tougher and more resilient than before, otherwise players I should never lose to would continue to pulverize me.

Don't ask me why, because I have never quite understood it myself – but once I decided to take up the challenge and fight my way out of the hole I was in, I began to play well again, and the very next season I started to show a bit of form. It's strange really, because, while I can look back on the 1987 British Open as the nadir of my professional career, it was that

defeat by Warren King that galvanized me into dis-
covering the will to win again.

The highpoint of the 1988 season for me was reaching
the final of the Mercantile Credit Classic at Norbreck
Castle Hotel, Blackpool. My opponent was Steve Davis
and, having gone ahead 11–10, I looked certain to go
two up with three frames to play. Then, in the 22nd
game, having made a break of 31, I missed a red I would
normally have pocketed without difficulty. It was the
only moment of the final that I failed to concentrate
totally on a shot and it cost me the tournament.

Steve had started the second day of the final holding
a 9–5 lead, having won six of the last seven frames the
night before. But then it was my turn to punish him. I
was very determined, starting with a clearance of 103
and following that with breaks of 58, 54, 44 and five
others of over 30. Now came that fatal mistake, and
Steve proceeded to clinch the title with breaks of 83,
68 and 99 for a 13–11 victory.

This defeat really knocked the stuffing out of me. I
felt psychologically gutted, my confidence blown away.
I returned home feeling very, very dejected. I don't
mind losing if I've given a tournament my best shot.
What undermined me was the knowledge that I'd
played terrific snooker for 99 per cent of the final, then
had thrown away the title with one irresponsible shot
at a critical point in the match. Champions, I told
myself, don't allow themselves to make that kind of
error.

Later, I analysed my performance and realized the
picture was nothing like as black as I had painted it.
Steve was still very much a winner, and the Mercantile

Credit Classic had provided him with his third victory from the four ranking events held so far that season. This was my first major final and I had given the world champion quite a fright, even though I still hadn't beaten him in what was our fourth professional engagement.

There were no more finals for me that season. I had to wait until the 1988–89 season, when the punishment started all over again: I finished runner-up in no less than four tournaments. The first of those was the 1988 World Matchplay at Brentwood. My opponent: Steve again! In the previous tournament, the UK Championship at Preston a couple of weeks before, Steve had beaten me 9–4 in the quarter-finals.

The World Matchplay involves the 12 players who obtained the most ranking points during the previous season. I was exempt until the quarter-finals, in which I defeated Joe Johnson 9–7 in an outstanding game; then I gained a 9–6 victory over Stephen Hendry to reach the final, which is played over 17 frames.

Once again I had to play second fiddle to Steve, who won the first six frames. I just couldn't peg back that deficit and lost 9–5. But I had the consolation of compiling the highest break of the tournament during the last session. This was 135, one more than the target Willie Thorne had set in the first round. Willie couldn't believe it when he arrived at the venue during the closing stages to find I had relieved him of £10,000 – the high-break prize.

Stephen Hendry was to deny me the 1989 Benson & Hedges Masters title at Wembley a month later, after I had beaten Dennis Taylor, Jimmy White and Neal

Foulds in the previous rounds. I lost 9–6 and for some reason I just didn't have the composure or ability at the table to stand back and say to myself: 'This is a good chance. Make the most of it.' I tended to rush my game, probably because of the tension and pressure I was under.

My next runner-up spot came in the final of the 1989 English Championship at Redwood Lodge, Bristol. I was beaten 9–7 by Mike Hallet. But this was a tremendous match to be involved in and I wasn't disappointed at losing. Mike had breaks of 105, 104, 75 and 62 to build up a 5–2 lead at the interval. He potted balls from everywhere. It was like trying to hold back the tide; I couldn't stop him. My own form was very consistent, however, and I was level with Mike after 14 frames. He had his third century of the final, a 108, to lead 7–4; then I had successive breaks of 56, 30, 66 and 105 to make it 7–7. Mike took the last two frames, compiling a break of 92 in the first of them. I was disappointed, of course, to be a runner-up again, but I was reasonably satisfied with my standard of play.

At the 1988 Benson & Hedges Masters semi-finals, Mike and myself had been involved in what I consider to be the most incredible frame of snooker I have ever played in. It was unreal and can only happen to you once in a lifetime. Mike had led 5–3 but I won the next two frames and in the decider built up a 65–26 points lead with only the colours left on the table. I was so excited at my recovery that after potting the last red I hit the green too hard. It bounced out of the back of the yellow pocket and on to the floor. So instead of being 46 points clear with only 27 on the table, my lead

60

was only 39. However, Mike still required at least four snookers and all the colours to win on the black.

From that moment, everything that could go wrong, went wrong, and I ended up losing. Once again, while Mike played well to get all those snookers and clear up from green to black, my own inexperience was painfully exposed. If I had shown any sort of composure I couldn't have lost, and I wasn't surprised Mike took a bit of a hammering from Steve Davis in the final: even Mike couldn't have believed his luck to win that last frame. No-one in professional snooker should win frames if they are 39 points behind on the colours. Even Mike's manager, Ian Doyle, and their 'roadie' John Carroll had given up when I potted the last red in the final frame. They shook hands with my friend Tony Shirley, who was sitting by them in the arena, wished us good luck in the final and went backstage, convinced their player was about to lose.

If nothing else that one frame taught me never to take liberties in a game of snooker. All I had to do after potting the last red was to play any simple safety shot I liked and Mike would have shaken hands – I don't think there's any doubt about that.

The 1989 Embassy World Championship marked my fourth defeat in a major final on home soil that season and fifth in all. Defeat number six came at the end of the year in the World Matchplay. This time I was beaten 18–9 by Jimmy White, who played as well as he has ever done against me. In the semi-finals I had recovered from losing the first five frames to beat Stephen Hendry 9–8, so I fancied my chances against Jimmy. I led 8–5 at one point, having had breaks of 111,

86 and 63, but Jimmy was level at 8–8 by the end of the first day of the two-day final. Only one frame fell to me on day two (though in that I had the consolation of a break of 102). But Jimmy was in full cry and breaks of 117, 100, 59, 50, 43 and 42 took him into a 15–9 lead with only one session to go. He didn't take long to finish me off, having further breaks of 45, 80 and 70.

Quite a performance that was from Jimmy. He seemed able to turn it on whenever he wanted to, and some of the pots he made were unreal.

The Benson & Hedges Masters final a month or so later was a repeat of 1989: John Parrott v Stephen Hendry. A 6–2 semi-final victory over Steve Davis the previous evening should have been the perfect preparation for me to avenge Stephen's victory of 12 months before. But in the last frame of the semi-final my tip split: it was virtually dust underneath the surface and had to be replaced. Normally that wouldn't present a problem – but I had left at home the small bottle in which I carry my cue tips. These are all old tips which have been bedded in during practice so that they are ready for use in matchplay. All I could do was fix on a brand new tip, which gave me absolutely no feel at all. It was like having a piece of marshmallow on the end of the cue, and every player knows you can't function properly with a tip in that condition. As it was, Stephen beat me comfortably by 9–4.

My apparent habit of losing in domestic finals was now beginning to get to me. Some of the papers were saying I had no bottle – yet it takes plenty of that, and willpower as well, even to get to the semi-finals in major tournaments. Many people also conveniently forgot that if you do keep losing in finals, the last thing you want to do is to reach another and lose again.

I had one last chance of a home victory right at the end of the 1989–90 season, but lost 4–2 to Stephen in the final of the Continental Airlines London Masters, a black-tie event staged at the Café Royal, London.

And so for the eighth time I was the bridesmaid. But at least I could comfort myself with the knowledge that I had to be consistently playing snooker of a high order to reach all these finals, so that it was just a matter of time before I won a tournament in front of my own supporters.

8

A Winner in Europe

Deauville, the French up-market resort on the Normandy coast, was the setting for my first worldranking-event title, the 1989 European Open. The tournament was held at the local casino, but it created hardly a whisper of interest. The locals are far more accustomed to the likes of Lester Piggott and Pat Eddery enjoying their hospitality than a bunch of snooker players.

Why on earth 64 of us had to make the trip to France remained a mystery. We knew it would be a cock-up from the word go; after all, the event was held in the heart of winter, when few people were likely to visit Deauville. The first two rounds of the European Open had been held at Blackpool. The top 32 players on the world ranking list were exempt until the third round, which started in Deauville on 30 January. (Nowadays, thank goodness, we play extra qualifying rounds at home venues and only 16 players go abroad. This makes things easy to organize and there is less hassle or expense for the players.)

My opponent, Eric Lawlor, had qualified for round three with victories over Jack Fitzmaurice and Ken

Owers; but then he decided to withdraw, which meant I didn't have to get to Deauville until the third day of the overseas stages. That saved me a few pennies because prices there were astronomical. I remember Les Dodd telling me it cost him £8 to ring home even though he failed to get through; while Jimmy White's steak and chips and a pint of lager set him back £55. (It's a good job Bill Werbeniuk didn't have to play there: lager cost a tenner a pint at the hotel we were staying at. Bill wouldn't have had much change left if he had won the tournament!)

Gary Wilkinson was my opponent in the fourth round, and after a 5–2 victory I faced Australia's John Campbell for a place in the quarter-finals. Only four people bothered to turn up to watch this match, so before the start I introduced them to the referee, John and myself and applauded them for coming. It wasn't the best-supported tournament in the world.

I had to wait five days in between beating John 5–0 in the fifth round and Eddie Charlton 5–1 in the quarter-finals because only one table instead of four was now being used. There was very little for us to do in our spare time because half the town had closed down until the holiday season began in the spring. To break the boredom I had the crosswords from the *Daily Mail* and one or two other papers faxed over to me, while some of the players had a kick-about on the beach.

Both Terry Griffiths and myself required the ninth and deciding frame to reach the final. Terry defeated Jimmy White 5–4 and I just managed to pip Mike Hallett, who had beaten Stephen Hendry in the quarter-finals.

I played steady snooker throughout the final. Terry led 4–1 but I was level after eight frames and held on to win 9–8 to capture my first major title. Perhaps Terry, who hadn't won a major for a few years, saw the winning post too soon. He led 5–4 and later 8–7, but I had a break of 106 in the 16th to tie the scores for the fourth time before winning the final frame 62–19.

It was a great feeling to win. It confirmed that I was doing the right things at last and could go all the way in a ranking tournament. My only disappointment was that all those who had supported me down the years were not around to see it. My wife Karen, manager Phil and close friend Tony Shirley – all of whom are usually at my matches – remained in England. Karen for once decided to stay at home, Phil was in hospital for treatment to an old neck injury, and Tony, who runs his own business, couldn't take the time off. I had to make a few phone calls that night.

A year later I retained my European title, this time in Lyon, France's third largest city, where the crowds were much better. So was the weather, as the event was held in March. Only 32 players made the trip to Lyon, which meant I had to play one round – the third – at Blackpool, where I won 5–1 against John Wright. The venue in Lyon was the Maison du Judo, a modern sports centre, which is not far from the gaol were Klaus Barbie, the infamous Nazi war criminal, is being held.

To reach the final I had to win four matches – against Wayne Jones (5–0), Joe Johnson (5–2), Nigel Bond (5–3), and Steve James (6–3). From the other half of the draw, Stephen Hendry came through unscathed, beating Steve Newbury (5–1), Tony Chappel (5–2), Neal Foulds (5–3), and Steve Davis (6–3).

I managed to beat Stephen 10–6 and was behind only once, at 5–6. I then won five in a row with breaks of 64, 57, 56, 42 (twice) and 41. To go ahead 9–6, I completed a clearance of 57 which enabled me to win on the black 65–60. Although it was not particularly difficult, it was at that time the best clearance under pressure that I had made in a final.

To beat Stephen was very satisfying. I'd had a tough draw which culminated in a final against a young man who at that time was the most devastating player in the game. He was a great rival then and will be for a long time to come.

If Deauville had been a bit of an end-of-pier event, lacking both credibility and excitement, Lyon was the genuine article – and proved I was a winner. The organization was first rate, and I think most people enjoyed the event, so full marks must go to Snooker Europe, who were the promoters of the 1990 event.

I think I showed a lot of character in that final. I could have chucked it in when Stephen led 6–5 – there have been times during my career when I didn't really put it in once I had fallen behind. But there was no way I was going to lose this one. I was in just the right frame of mind – relaxed, determined, and able to concentrate totally on the job every time I went to the table. It was unquestionably the best performance of my professional career until I won the world title at Sheffield.

Karen, Phil and Tony were in Lyon, which made my victory even more acceptable. We rang my Dad up to tell him the result, and we sang down the phone to him – he must have thought we were all drunk. Tony enjoyed every minute; it was the first time he had been with us on an away trip. He has been a friend of mine since I was about 17 and came into the Parrott 'team' in about 1985. My results at the time were not all that good and Phil agreed with me that a new face might not be a bad idea. Moreover, Phil was finding it difficult to be with me at every tournament, so in his absence Tony's support was a godsend. Soon Tony became an essential part of the set-up. He has proved a good friend, a good influence, and the right person to have around when the chips are down.

Talking of the Parrott team, when Karen, Phil, Tony and myself arrived at Lyon airport, Steve Davis (who had just come in on another flight) looked over the Arrivals balcony and called out: 'Blimey, the Liverpool connection! You'll have to win the tournament just to cover your expenses.' Which is exactly what I did.

I didn't stay up too late after completing my European Open double and enjoyed a good night's sleep. The next morning I was up early and went to wake Phil. It turned out that he, thinking he ought to celebrate on my behalf as well as his own, had managed to force a few liquid refreshments down his throat and had been unable to get to bed before 5.30. He'd been in bed for only an hour when I sounded the reveille, and when he tried to put his trousers on, he missed with one leg, attacked the bedside table with his head, and ended in a tangle on the floor. I remind him of this occasionally.

My next victory in Europe came in the 1990 Humo Belgian Masters, a Barry Hearn eight-man tournament held in Antwerp. I defeated Jimmy White 9–6 in a marvellous final before quite a big crowd, following a 5–1 victory over Terry Griffiths in the first round and a 5–3 win against Stephen Hendry in the semi-finals.

The table used was a little easier than some of those we have had to play on in England – the pockets were a little more forgiving – and this made for very exciting snooker. I made a break of 120 in the 13th frame to go with breaks of 94, 84, 76, 71, 60, 59, 53, and 52. Jimmy wasn't hanging about either, with breaks of 104, 96, 75 and 53.

Again it was a very satisfying tournament for me and I was very proud to get my hands on another trophy. It was just a bit frustrating to think I had now won three times in Europe but not once in England. Oddly enough, I was also on my own in Belgium, the only other occasion on which this has happened during my professional career.

The Norwich Union Grand Prix was the last of the four tournaments I won in Europe between February 1989 and October 1990. This gave me a clean sweep of all the European titles played for during that period. The first round of this event was held in Paris at the studios of Canal Plus, the French pay-network TV. I defeated Jimmy White 4–1 and during the match compiled what was to be the highest break of the event, a 138. Subsequent rounds were played at Monte Carlo, one of my favourite resorts, in the opulent surroundings of the Metropole Palace Hotel. Stephen Hendry, Steve Davis and the holder Joe Johnson were also involved in the semi-final stages.

I was drawn against Stephen in the semis and won

an uninspiring match 4–2, while Steve beat Joe 4–3. The final wasn't brilliant either, but I won 4–2 after Steve had taken two of the first three frames. For me the chief satisfaction lay in the fact that I had beaten Steve in a final for the first time. Moreover, I had drawn the short straw in the invited entry of eight because to win I had had to beat the number one, two and four seeds. It was the strangest draw I have ever seen.

I received five trophies: one each for winning, shot of the night, shot of the tournament, highest break and highest break of the night. Snooker Europe, the promoter, had provided trophies for just about everything, and I was lucky enough to win most of them. Karen, Phil and his wife Jean were with me in Monte, and we had some fun carrying the hardware back to England.

9

Karen & Me

The Parrotts – that's Karen and me – live about 100 yards from Strawberry Fields, the home for orphans immortalized by the Beatles. Before I was married, Dad and I had a house about the same distance from Penny Lane. I suppose the next logical step is to go and live near Abbey Road in London to complete the Fab Four connection.

I first met Karen at the Walton Hospital club, where I went with Tony Shirley one Friday evening. I'd played that same day in the Lada Classic at Warrington and did reasonably well, even though I lost 5–4 to Steve Davis in the semi-finals. On returning to Liverpool Tony, who had a couple of mates working on the door of the club, suggested we went there for a drink or two. I wasn't too keen but in the end gave in to Tony's powers of persuasion.

Inside the club I happened to catch sight of this vision who walked by me in a striped dress. I made a few discreet inquiries in the right quarters and I discovered that her name was Karen.

I remember our first date very well. I met her off the bus and we went to a London Road pub in the city centre. Karen never stopped talking all evening, but I knew from the outset we were meant for each other – she was great company, very intelligent, and I fancied her like mad!

Karen is a couple of years younger than me. She worked as a medical secretary at the Royal Hospital in Liverpool. When we first met she was still at college, but she happened to be one of those 'brain boxes' at shorthand and obtained a job at the hospital with relative ease having reached a speed of 140 words per minute. Karen worked there for five years, eventually giving up full-time work at the hospital when we got married. She could have stayed on: the choice was hers. But she decided to leave and become a lady of leisure – though occasionally she goes back on a temporary basis if they are short of staff at the hospital.

One of the hardest things I have ever done in my life was to ask Karen's parents for their consent to our marriage. We went with them one Sunday night to the Queen's Restaurant on Queen's Drive in Old Swan. Nothing unusual about that – we often took them out for a drink on a Sunday. But on this particular evening I'd decided that, having allowed two earlier opportunities to pass, this had to be the point of no return.

By now, of course, Karen was accusing me of cowardice and anything else she could think of. But after three or four rounds of drinks at the Queen's I eventually picked up enough courage to say to her parents, 'Look, there's something I want to tell you.'

At this, Karen's mum looked aghast. I think she was convinced I was going to tell her that her daughter was pregnant. However, I pressed on, finally getting to the gist of the matter: 'We want to get married. Is it alright with you?'

Karen's mum burst into tears straight away. Her dad was brilliantly cool, waiting a second or two before turning to me and saying: 'Well, it's your round then, son.'

I had no answer to that.

They have always been a very friendly family and they made me welcome at their home from the day I began courting Karen. She is the eldest of the three children; she has a brother Tony and a younger sister Janine. Their home was 5.1 miles from my own house: I know the exact distance because I set the mileage trip on the car to check it.

Most of the time we were courting our relationship was pretty good. We had the occasional arguments, and there were times when we didn't see each other for a while – but that was only because I had a job which took me away from home quite a lot. Our rows were never anything really serious. We always knew we would be together one day and that's the way it has turned out. We are absolutely madly and passionately in love.

We were married at St Paul's Church in West Derby, on 3 June 1989. The priest, Father Adrian, has become a great friend of ours, and while we haven't seen him for a while we never forget to send him a bottle of wine at Christmas.

I had to go with Karen to see him in the weeks leading up to the wedding and, between explaining to us the religious side of marriage, we had any number of laughs with him. And of course after each visit we would take him to the local for a couple of swift halves.

Father Adrian, a former customs and excise officer, is a terrific man who has a great sense of humour. He loves the Marx Brothers and we talked a lot about their old black and white films. He's very keen on snooker and likes to play when he can find the time. I was still at CueMasters at the time of the wedding and Stephen Hendry, Mike Hallett and Darren Morgan all came to the church and the reception afterwards.

I'd already booked our honeymoon in Mauritius when I bumped into Steve Davis at the Café Royal. He asked me where we were going to and it turned out we had chosen the hotel he had once stayed at. He considered it to be the best one on the island. I have to admit I'd picked this hotel only because it was the one in the brochure that appealed most of all to me. But Steve was right.

Before the wedding one major problem cropped up: whether I would be available to play in the Australian Open (which at the 11th hour had been switched to Hong Kong to become the Hong Kong Open) and the Dubai Duty Free Classic, two overseas world ranking events for the 1989–90 season. Phil had already pulled me out of another overseas ranking event, the Asian Open, and when the dates for the third round matches of the Hong Kong and Dubai events were suddenly changed, I nearly pulled out of those as well.

What a predicament to be in! Here I was getting married on 3 June while on 5 June I was due to play in the third round of the Hong Kong Open and on 11 June I had a third round game in the Dubai Duty Free Classic – both matches to be played at sunny Blackpool.

Our honeymoon in Mauritius was due to start on 4 June.

After long discussion, Karen and I decided it was more prudent to postpone the honeymoon for one week to enable me to play in the qualifiers as scheduled. It was a miracle that the honeymoon dates could be altered. In a nutshell, the first week was tagged on to the end of the second week, so I was able to play and beat Matt Gibson in the Hong Kong Open and Paul Gibson in the Dubai Duty Free Classic and qualify for the overseas stages of both events.

The flight to Mauritius was a long one, 16 hours in all, but the hotel was superb. It was on its own private island and had two restaurants and a beautiful beach: all very quiet but as near to paradise as anyone would want.

While Karen and myself revelled in the sun and surf at this Indian Ocean dream, our home in Liverpool was undergoing extensive changes. It was the house I had shared with my father after we left Ramilies Road. Dad always said he would move out if I wanted to live there when I got married, though at the outset Karen and I looked high and low for somewhere else.

In the end and after eight long months of fruitless searching, we came to the conclusion that there wasn't anywhere any better. The house was ripped to pieces (apart from the snooker room) and restyled in the way Karen wanted. I bought another, smaller house for my Dad about a mile and a half away. He is a very independent man and lives on his own, but he is close enough for me to keep an eye on him.

Karen could make a good living as an interior

designer. Though she's my wife, I have to say she has marvellous taste – the house is now altogether classier and much more stylish than ever before.

She selected all the colour schemes. She was a little sneaky as well: when I returned home after my first-round match in the 1991 Embassy World Championship, the house had been completely wallpapered – yet I'd only been away for three days. Karen never told me anything about it, she just went out and set everything up, even to the extent of helping out herself.

When we first moved into the house we didn't have a kitchen for three weeks. All we had was a tap coming out of the wall; there were no units or anything like that. The snooker room was in a right mess; you couldn't pot a black off its spot because of the furniture that was stored in there during the renovations. Obviously this upset my practice routines, because I just wasn't able to put in the amount of work I would have liked.

It must have taken about six months to complete the work on the house; even so, it was carried out in double-quick time because I wanted it done and out of the way as soon as possible.

Funnily enough, when I originally bought the house in September 1985 the chap who was involved in selling it didn't know me from Adam. I hadn't shaved for three days, and with a hole in my jeans where the snooker chalk used to go, I probably looked rather like a tramp when I enquired about the asking price. Only the footings and foundations were completed at the time, and I could see that this fellow was confident he would frighten me off when he told me that the prices started at £80,000.

I had Phil with me, and when I told the salesman we would be back in a couple of days time, I'm sure he thought he would never see us again. But back we went – and on our second visit the salesman was as nice as pie, even though we haggled with him about the price. And when I told him I wanted a snooker room at the front, that was no problem either: the footings and foundations would be dug up and replaced, he said.

It was a struggle for me to get that sort of money together in 1985; but Phil told me not to worry, if I wanted the house I could have it and should leave the details to him. I was lucky enough to have a couple of decent tournaments that year; the prize money helped a great deal towards the purchase price. I was certainly cleaned out by the time the transaction went through. But, thanks to Phil's advice, I consider it now to be the best investment I ever made.

We've had lots of things done to the house since we got married but everything which had to be done has been done so there are no worries at all and that's a nice position to be in. I even had a new snooker table installed last year. It's wonderful to be in a position where you don't have to worry about where the next penny is coming from. It seems to me 9 out of 10 problems in most marriages come from financial troubles.

Children? We are enjoying life too much on our own to be ready yet for the sound of tiny feet in the Parrott household. We have talked about it often and have agreed that one day, yes – but not just yet. It's up to Karen if and when we have any children, because she will have to do all the hard work. (If child bearing was left to us fellows, I don't think there would be all that many kids knocking about.)

We both love children and often take out Karen's two little cousins, seven-year-old Tom and four-year-old Lorraine. We take them on day trips here and there. On one occasion I wished I hadn't. I'd just collected my car from being cleaned and valetted, and Lorraine was sick all over her brother on the back seat.

What a performance! She could have aimed anywhere, but she chose to be sick all over her brother, who was wearing his new track suit. The smell seemed to linger in the car for weeks afterwards.

10

Pressure at the Crucible: Hillsborough and After

The Hillsborough tragedy occurred the day before I played Steve James in the first round of the 1989 Embassy World Championship. Hillsborough, Sheffield Wednesday's stadium, is situated only a couple of miles from the Crucible Theatre where, at the time of the catastrophe on the Leppings Lane terracing, the two afternoon snooker matches were about to start.

I had gone with friends to Villa Park in Birmingham to watch the other FA Cup semi-final in which Everton defeated Norwich City 1–0, though I can't remember anything about the second half. Once the full impact of what was happening at Hillsborough had reached us, nothing else seemed to matter. It was so traumatic, it left me numb. I was with Tony Shirley and Roy Edwards, who are both true-blue Everton supporters. But Roy's two lads had gone to Hillsborough, where their favourites Liverpool were playing Nottingham Forest.

It was an agonizing time for Roy, who was desperate to find out if his boys were safe. Everyone was looking for telephones, but that's one of the many amenities our soccer grounds conspicuously lack. We could see what had happened at Hillsborough by turning round where we were standing and watching the television set inside the executive box behind us. The scenes were horrific. I'd grown up on The Kop and there were scores of Liverpool supporters being rushed away on improvised stretchers made from the advertising hordings around the touchline. Liverpool is a very close knit community: we all felt an instinctive solidarity, a communal sorrow that afternoon and for weeks to come.

Thankfully Roy found out later his sons were safe. Thankfully no direct relatives of mine or my wife's was injured, although I knew several people who had lost a loved one among the 95 who died that afternoon. When I arrived home I rang Phil, who told me his own son Duncan had been at Hillsborough, but he was fairly sure he had a stand seat. He called me back later to say Duncan had rung and was quite safe.

I wore a black armband when I played Steve for a place in the last 16 at the Crucible. Just before I went out to play, Phil chatted to me about the tragic events of the previous day. He pointed out that sometimes one can draw strength from adversity, and he urged me to try and play for all the people of Liverpool.

And what an incredible match it turned out to be. It was voted the match of the season by the other players and Steve and myself each received a trophy. I certainly didn't see anything better that season, and as far as I was concerned it was a pleasure to have taken part and to be honoured for it by my fellow professionals.

I know Steve really fancied playing me and I really fancied playing him. A mutual friend of ours had been

Doing my Jesse James routine.

On my way to Dovedale Road school, aged five.

I don't think Willie Carson will lose any sleep over this riding style!

In my old Everton kit in Wavertree Park, 1972.

With Neal Foulds on tour in Zimbabwe. Alex Thomson (*left*) was our charitable host and Stan Brooke (*right*) from the B&SCC was our guide and mentor.

Signing my first cue contract with Peradon and Fletcher, under the watchful eye of my manager Phil Miller (*right*).

The first major victory of my career, the Pontin's Open Championship, 1982.

With Ray Reardon and the 'Great WT', after winning the Astra Silver Cue Pro-Am, 1982.

An early photo with Steve Davis in a BBC Television studio. Little did I know that we would have some great matches in the following years.

With Phil after receiving the Young Player of the Year Award, 1984.

My Alma Mater, the Dudley Institute. Note the painted windows –
curtains weren't good enough!

With playing partner Dave Williams after my first 147 break.

1ST NOVEMBER 1984

After the 1989 final with champ Steve Davis and referee Len Ganley. (*David Muscroft Snooker Library*)

Success in Lyon. Winding down with my old friend Tony Shirley and Karen after a great week's work, March 1990.

Back home with my Dad ('The Colonel') after Lyon.

Scenes from the 1991 Embassy World Championship. *Top*: Concentration etched deep in my face. *Bottom*: Jimmy White looks on. (*David Muscroft Snooker Library*)

saying I didn't think I was going to lose and Steve didn't think he was going to lose either. So the two of us came out like a couple of stags and really locked antlers in the Crucible. I had three century breaks – 110, 103 and 102 – yet when I had completed the last of those, Steve was leading 7–6. A break of 62 helped me to draw level, and after winning the 15th frame I went on to lead 9–7 on the black. Steve won the next two frames – the second of which was also a black ball finish – before I managed to squeeze into the second round by taking the decider 56–22.

I still have bits of this match on video. In nearly every frame in which I broke off, Steve knocked in a red, and twice he swerved out of a snooker to do so. It was breathtaking stuff.

My next match was against Dennis Taylor, and again it was a tough one. I had a break of 104 in the opening frame, but Dennis played very well to lead 7–6 and then 10–9. I put my best foot forward in the remaining frames to win 13–10, and that was a good last session for me.

Jimmy White followed in the quarter-finals. He had beaten me at Sheffield 13–8 in 1986 and 13–11 a year later. I knew I had a better chance of winning this one because I was much more experienced now and recently had had a fairly good record against him. He is always a difficult opponent, but this time I fairly roared out of the trap to lead 7–1. Jimmy got back to 8–6, but I won five of the last six frames to take the match 13–7. No century breaks this time but I managed three of 80-plus and six more between 40 and 65. You have to be on your best form to beat Jimmy at the Crucible.

To reach the final I now had to beat Tony Meo.

81

He didn't play well at all and must have been very disappointed after having got so far in the championship. My play was nothing to shout about either. I won 16–7, but I had the depressing feeling that, after my terrific performances in the previous rounds, I was mentally and physically running out of fuel. I had played in 11 tournaments before Sheffield, reaching some six finals, three semi-finals and two quarter-finals; and then there was the trauma of Hillsborough.

As for the final, it was a disaster as far as I was concerned. Steve Davis was bidding for his sixth championship and he pulverized me – which is what he was there to do. By the time the score had reached 10–2 I just wanted to get out of the place as soon as I could: I knew I was not going to win from that position.

In the end I lost 18–3, and one of the hardest things about it was that afterwards I was told by the tournament director, Paul Hatherell, that I would have to go back out in the evening and do an exhibition with Steve because the match had finished with a session to spare. Now, who wants to play an exhibition after suffering the heaviest defeat in the history of World Championship finals? I certainly didn't, and I thought it was pretty tactless to ask me to do so. Phil tried to reason with members of the board of the WPBSA, pointing out that I was mentally exhausted and shouldn't be forced to play. He was told I could be fined if I didn't. He got scant support from people who we had expected to be sympathetic.

In the end the exhibition turned out to be a good laugh. Nigel Oldfield, who is on the staff of the WPBSA, came out dressed in an ape suit, the soda syphons were used indiscriminately, and the match table was completely ruined. I told a few gags and basically worked my way through it on autopilot. Barry Hearn watched the fun and games for a time with Phil and told him I had shown a lot of bottle going out to play. Phil formed the impression that Steve would not have done so in similar circumstances. I received a number of letters which congratulated me on my attitude. I want the people who wrote those letters to know how grateful I was to receive them and how they helped me get over the hiding I had suffered.

Later that evening I returned home with Karen, who could see how I felt. She is very understanding – but it must have been just as disappointing for her, especially as she had brought along a friend and her boyfriend to watch the final. I didn't go out for a fortnight. I wanted so badly to win for Liverpool, but in the end I was shattered; I didn't want to know anyone, I didn't want to see anyone. It wasn't owing to any embarrassment at the size of my defeat: I was psychologically knackered and seemed to lack the emotional and physical energy to get up out of my chair.

Weeks after the final Phil realized I'd had enough snooker for a while, and he withdrew me from an event in Belgium and from the world-ranking Asian Open, which was to be played that summer in Bangkok. I was fined £200 for withdrawing from the Asian, but having that time off helped me regain my appetite for the game. Once again I was thankful I had a manager who understood me and put me first. Needless to say the know-alls criticized him for this, but Phil knew best of all how much I needed a break.

A year later I returned to the Crucible for another shot at the world title. I almost went out in the first round to Mark Bennett – and a defeat then, at the scene of my annihilation by Steve, could have left a permanent scar on my game. It was an incredibly tough match, with Mark potting balls from all over the place. He obviously had a game plan to go for everything, and it nearly came off. He didn't make any startling breaks – his highest was only 38 compared with the eight I had between 54 and 84 – but he still led 5–2, 7–6, and 9–7.

My most important break was a clearance of 69, which took me to a 10–9 victory on the black after Mark had led 59–0 in the 19th frame. I was very proud of that break; it was one of my best ever and most timely clearances. And Mark, who had seemed about to slam the door in my face, must have been very disappointed – especially since, if he had won the match, he would have been in the top 32 of the world ranking list the following season.

It was a needle match when I played Dean Reynolds for a place in the quarter-finals. He can be a great lad, but sometimes he can be a bit funny as well. The needle was there before the start and continued throughout the match. It stemmed from some comments Dean had made at the Grosvenor Hotel, where we were both staying. I didn't actually hear what was said. It was told to me at second hand by a reliable witness; and as it happened by the bar, I imagine the beer was doing some of the talking. But I wasn't too happy about a couple of the things Dean was reported to have said.

He also made the odd comment during the match,

which didn't improve my mood. I probably went into the press conference too soon after I had won 13–11. I was very annoyed, and I might not have said what I did had I taken advantage of the 10-minute cooling-down rule. It did not help either that both of us were more hyped up than usual because at the end of the third session we had been pulled off at 12–11, when there were at most only two more frames to play.

At the press conference I spoke my mind honestly. At that moment Dean wasn't exactly my flavour of the month; and while I didn't want a punch-up with him, I didn't want to go out for a pint with him either. Things certainly got out of hand, with Dean saying he had lost a lot of respect for me as a player. So at the start of the following season I went up to him and apologized for any comments I had made that might have offended him. Dean expressed similar sentiments because he didn't want to fall out with me. Since then everything has been amicable. We probably get on better now than we have ever done.

I went on to beat Cliff Thorburn 13–6 for a place in the semi-finals. During that match I compiled the highest break of the tournament, a 140 in the 12th frame, to lead 8–4.

Funny the way that break came along, because it was during one of the worst sessions I have ever been involved in. Cliff went to the toilet at the end of the 11th frame, and I said to the referee John Street. 'Not a very good game is it?' John replied, a touch drily: 'You know when you have potted a red? Well, you take a colour next.' When Cliff came back it was his turn to break off – and that was the only time he went to the table in that frame.

I couldn't wait to get my own back when I had finished the total clearance. I turned to John and asked: 'Is that what you're supposed to do?'

Next came Stephen Hendry, and this was also a somewhat peculiar match, with first one player and then the other in front. I took the first session 5–3 and Stephen the second 6–1 to lead 9–6, but after 22 frames we were level at 11–11. I didn't win another frame in the last session and never looked like doing so, and Stephen took the match 16–11. During that final session the pressure was greater than I had ever experienced. It wasn't just affecting me: Stephen said it was pressure with a capital P, and he wasn't kidding. I can't remember potting a ball. Stephen had handed me two frames on a plate but I threw the chances away. It was a sickener at the time. But while I went away feeling gutted by my performance in that last session, I felt I would learn something from this match that would stand me in good stead when I got into the same position again.

11

A Near Miss

Monday 14 January 1991 is a day I'll never forget. I'm lucky to be alive to tell the tale – and so is Phil. I had called round for him that morning in plenty of time for us to drive to the National Exhibition Centre in Birmingham where I was due to play Jack McLaughlin in the first round of the World Masters men's singles. This was a brand new £1 million tournament run on similar lines to the tennis at Wimbledon and was televised by Sky TV. There were 12 tables in all, with 10 located around the perimeter of the arena and the other two situated back-to-back in central positions. These were the two main match tables, on which the television coverage concentrated.

Phil and myself had set out four hours before the scheduled start of play. I didn't know at the time whether my match would begin at 2pm or would be one of those which went on a little later in the afternoon.

I never drive to tournaments, so Phil took the wheel of my BMW and we set off for Birmingham via the M56 and M6. Traffic was light on the M56, but as we left it to join the M6 southbound, we could see that there was a huge traffic jam. (It turned out that a lorry had shed its load some four miles further south and the tailback now stretched as far as the M56 intersection.)

We had just crawled into the nearside lane of the M6 when a 38-ton juggernaut came thundering along behind us from the M56 slip road. Phil glanced into his driving mirror and realized that danger was imminent: the truck was swerving from side to side as it headed towards us and seemed unable to stop.

The slow lane of the M6 was chock-a-block with vehicles which were hardly moving; the middle lane offered us a chance of reaching safety only if a gap appeared in the traffic. To stay in the nearside lane however would mean certain death. The juggernaut was bearing down on us at about 50 mph: the driver had either dozed off or his brakes had gone. Phil shouted to me, 'The bugger isn't going to stop!'

At the very last second the lorry driver seemed to get some action from his brakes, while Phil somehow edged halfway into the middle lane – and that saved our lives.

The lorry driver was very brave: as his truck started to skid, he chose to swerve left and went careering down the motorway embankment rather than ramming another juggernaut ahead of him. Our car had been between the two trucks – the meat in the sandwich! – but with Phil able to manoeuvre towards the middle lane, it gave the approaching lorry driver the chance to avoid total disaster. As it was, his truck clouted the nearside backend of the BMW as it passed us. At the bottom of the embankment, the truck's wheels became half embedded in mud, such was the speed it had been travelling at. The impact shunted the BMW into the middle lane of the motorway, and it was a miracle that we didn't hit another vehicle.

By now the traffic had stopped and Phil was able to get the car to the safety of the hard shoulder. I got out of the car and felt a bit stiff around the neck – having been warned what might happen, I had braced myself for the collision. The lorry driver, who was from Scotland, scrambled up the embankment. It was obvious he was in a state of shock, and he kept repeating over and over that his brakes had locked. Frankly, I was more worried about him than about us. He asked if we were all right and on learning no one had been hurt, remarked on the state of the BMW. I told him it was only metal and could be repaired.

The police arrived to take down the necessary details. Fortunately they were able to give us the go-ahead to continue our journey because our rear brake lights were still working, even though the boot of the car had buckled under the force of the impact. When we told them where we were going and that time was running short, they escorted us, with blue light flashing, as far as the next exit on the M6. We then followed a diversionary route which took us beyond the original tailback and on to the motorway.

A message that we had been involved in an accident was also relayed by the police to the tournament office at the NEC, and when we eventually arrived I was relieved to be told that my match with Jack McLaughlin had been re-scheduled for a little later in the afternoon.

Phil and myself examined the damage to the car more thoroughly when he parked it at the NEC. The boot had been knocked into a triangular shape and the lid would not open. To get hold of my cue and dress suit, I had to put my arm through a hole and pull them out. (A proper examination of the car later revealed no damage to the chassis. This was due to the height of the truck's bumper, which made the impact. A lower vehicle might have caused much greater damage. As it was, repairs took five weeks to complete at a cost of £5000.)

I realized the media were aware of what had happened when Phil was called to a press conference the moment we walked into the NEC, so my first priority was to phone Karen and tell her I was still in one piece. The last thing I wanted was for her to find out from a radio news bulletin or some other source that I had been involved in a crash on the M6.

When I look back I realize how lucky Phil and I were not to have been killed. All the bad run of the balls I have moaned about over the years pale into insignificance when I think about that crash. I remember Phil saying to me, 'God's looking after us, he must have spared us for something. Maybe you'll win the World Championship this year.'

12

Back to Basics

I knew I was playing well enough to have a chance of
winning the 1991 Embassy World Championship some
five weeks before my first match against Nigel Gilbert.
January, February and March had been a disaster from
a playing point of view. I had been experiencing big
trouble with my cue. It was affecting my confidence;
and since 95 per cent of this game is in the mind, I had
to do something about it.

Eventually I managed to find a cue I liked. It was
made by Hunt & O'Byrne, who are based near the
Elephant and Castle in London. I was able to pop into
their showrooms because at the time I was doing a
photo session at Riley's, the cue manufacturers, whose
premises are just across the road. Jimmy White was
also involved in the promotional work.

The cue in question was one the firm had on sale. I
picked it up and had a good look at it. I told Will Hunt,
the man in charge, that it seemed to be quite a nice cue
but that for me it was a little on the thin side at the tip
end. After I left, Mr Hunt took the cue away, cut it,
tapered it, and spliced on a new butt. My old cue was
living on borrowed time after I had lost 5–1 to Eddie

Charlton in the third round of the Mercantile Credit Classic at the beginning of the year. It nearly was the first whitewash of my career – I had managed to avoid that by winning the fifth frame. Eddie deserved to win, he played very well; but once again I didn't perform anywhere near the best of my ability. It was my worst spell for several years – and a lousy preparation for the World Championship in a few months' time. (It's true I managed to win a match in the Benson & Hedges Masters at Wembley a few weeks later – but only because Willie Thorne had the kindness to play even worse than I did.)

The Pearl Assurance British Open at Derby was the next world-ranking event, and once again round three (the first round I had to play in) put me among the also rans. I lost this time to Colin Roscoe. I was continuing in the same dreadful form and he punished me severely. The run of poor results had eroded my confidence, and when that happens your luck flies out of the window and it's your opponents who always seem to be favoured by the rub of the green. This is not to take anything away from Colin, who played really well and thoroughly deserved to take his place in the next round.

I knew now that my old cue was finished. For one or two seasons it had been all right; but while the shaft was not altered, new butts and joints had been fitted, and this changed the balance of the cue. I'm glad I got rid of it when I did.

Three days after losing to Colin, Phil came round to my house to express his views on my current form. I had, he felt, temporarily lost the capacity to rely on my two main assets, natural ability and instinct. He said he was fed up watching me play snooker in a manner that was against my basic nature. It looked as if I was playing myself instead of the balls. I saw the sense in what he was saying, and we discussed the best way for me to return to the way I used to play.

There was only one answer: we had to isolate ourselves in my snooker room and get down to some very serious practice. The World Championship was only five weeks away; and before that came the Benson & Hedges Irish Masters. So now came a period of hard graft and total concentration as I set about rediscovering how I used to play at the Golden Leisure Snooker Centre in Liverpool. It was the way Dad had always wanted me to play. It was a return to the basics.

For several years I'd been coached by Frank Callan (a former Blackpool fishmonger). I'll always be grateful for the help and advice he gave me, which in purely technical terms was excellent. I think possibly, though, he tried to take me too deep into theory – which for other players would have been fine but which seemed to get in the way of my natural instinct.

I had a terrific initial boost because it was immediately obvious that my new cue was an absolute cracker: it was properly weighted, beautifully balanced, and above all had that special feel about it that you can't describe but you know at once if it's there.

I held the cue exactly the way I used to, started splitting the balls up and – lo and behold – all of a sudden, my old confidence came flooding back. I was starting to play again – and I was not worrying about anything.

After a week or so Phil knew I was starting to loosen

up and regain my fluency. I was clearing my mind of everything that could confuse it – and I was potting everything in sight. Both of us couldn't have been more pleased at the way things were beginning to shape up. More practice followed, and after another week I was feeling so good in myself that when Phil opened the balls and left me a red, I was clearing the table practically every time. My cue felt part of me and I knew it was the one I had always wanted.

The Benson & Hedges Irish Masters was the next event, and I was now looking forward to it so much I couldn't wait for it to start. I also knew that no one apart from those closest to me was aware that I had fully recovered my confidence and form. Goffs, which is in County Kildare on the Naas road from Dublin, is a unique and marvellous setting for snooker. The B & H Irish Masters is held there each year, and it was a blessing to me that it was so close to the World Championship, which would begin some two weeks after the Irish final.

My first game was an awkward one against Nigel Bond. There was a lot of pressure on me because I knew my new-found confidence had yet to be justified by victory in match play.

Nigel was by no means an easy draw, but I managed to win 5–3, and this was just the boost I needed. Dennis Taylor followed, and after a 6–2 victory I went on to lose 9–5 to Steve Davis in the final.

I wasn't too dismayed about this result. For one thing, both Steve and I knew the match was much closer than the score suggests, and I had fought back to level the scores at the end of the eighth frame after

94

losing the first four. However, Steve went on to play two immaculate frames from 5–5 and pulled away.

I thought Steve played reasonably well, but I knew myself that I wasn't quite 100 per cent. It was like when a footballer comes back after a long lay-off through injury: he may be perfectly physically fit but he's not yet match fit. The important thing for me was that my game was beginning to return and that I was going about things the right way. And when we returned home to Liverpool it was back to the snooker room to carry on where we had left off. I had a lot more belief in myself and was looking forward to Sheffield and the World Championship.

By the time Sheffield was only a week away, I was absolutely buzzing and so full of confidence I found it hard to believe how I had been playing only four or five weeks earlier.

It was arranged for Tony Shirley, my closest friend, to come to Sheffield with us. Phil had explained to him what had been going on and he knew only too well there must be no distractions. It gave me a big lift to realize that Phil was convinced I had a real chance of winning. In fact, he wanted to back me to win and took the money with him to the Crucible – only to be persuaded by John Spencer there was no point in having a bet: the benefits of winning would far out-weigh anything else.

13

Champion of the World

The bookmakers rated me a 16–1 chance before the start of the 1991 Embassy World Championship, which was being played for the 15th successive year at the Crucible Theatre, Sheffield.

The gentlemen at the *Racing Post* had their own ideas about my chances in their championship preview. Summing up, they reckoned I had had a bad season – partly true – couldn't possibly be backed, and in general was one to avoid. If I had been a horse I would have had two Timeform squiggles, not one, in their form guide. I'm always amused by what they have to say. I was chuckling to myself this time because they seemed to be about two months behind in their assessment of my form. The chance to show that their oracle was on the blink gave me a bit of an extra boost – not that I needed it.

At Sheffield we booked in as usual at the Grosvenor Hotel. It's the perfect place to stay as far as I'm concerned: it's just a short walk to the Crucible, which gives you the chance to gulp a few lungfuls of fresh air before plunging into the windowless arena. As it turned out, I returned home for three days between the first and second rounds, but thereafter remained at the hotel until the end. I went home to practise. With 32 players involved in the first round and 16 in the second, it is extremely difficult to get on the Crucible's practice table. But at home I could practise as much as I wanted to in a peaceful environment.

That first match against Nigel Gilbert brought me a 10–6 victory which was not quite as easy as the score-line might suggest. Nigel is a good player whose results so far haven't done him justice. I was very impressed by his performance and the way he hung in there. He also potted several shot-to-nothing balls, and I don't remember him missing many long balls throughout the match. In fact, I was a bit fortunate to lead 6–3 overnight. There were a couple of close frames and I remember clearing up with a break of 32 to win the second on the black, having needed three snookers.

I think all the players are wary of the first round at the World Championship. You hope to have a good tournament, but you don't feel you are really in it until that opening match is over. There was also extra pressure on me because, if I had lost to Nigel, Neal Foulds (who had already won his opening match) would push me out of the top four on the world ranking list.

When I went home I was feeling pretty content at having won. I had had breaks of 131, 95 and 87; but it wasn't the breaks so much as the way I was hitting the ball that pleased me. My safety play, which had been a bit ropy throughout the season, had also improved; it wasn't marvellous in this match but it was a great deal better than it had been. If I could maintain the way I was potting, I knew my safety would get even better.

Since Sheffield, friends have commented on how well I was using the rest. I'd not noticed that, probably because I've never been frightened of it. You think about the rest only if you don't like using it. Dennis Taylor, for instance, is one of the finest players in the world, yet on his own admission he hates using the rest. That's why, whenever possible, he will avoid using it by playing left-handed. I can't understand why a player of his ability doesn't like using the rest. It's part and parcel of the game – in fact, I sometimes deliberately play shots to leave myself having to use the rest. I know it is the right shot to play. In similar circumstances, however, Dennis will often fiddle around the table to get on to some other, inferior ball which allows him to avoid using the rest.

My next opponent was Tony Knowles, who had beaten John Virgo 10–8 despite losing the first four frames. The first of our three scheduled sessions was at times rather iffy. I won the first frame on the black, cleared up with a break of 79 to win the second 79–50, and went in 3–1 at the interval. Yet I could just as easily have been 3–1 down.

My lead had stretched to 7–1 by the end of the first session and Phil, Tony Shirley and I agreed that, if I could win with a session to spare, it would provide a further boost to my confidence – and also give me a day off to relax.

I had already made a break of 137, and I followed that with a 138 before running out a 13–1 winner. Tony and I spent my day off at Pontefract races – in the pouring rain. Ray Edmonds, the BBC commentator who is also a professional, told me to back a certain horse in the first race. It may still be running, or it may be back between the shafts of a milk float. But apart from that it was a good day out.

By now I felt I was playing 21 points better than the bookmakers had suggested in their pre-championship betting – though when I said as much after beating Tony it was probably another little jibe at my friends at the *Racing Post*. I wasn't being boastful either; it really was the way I felt. I knew that, whoever I was playing, if he gave me the slightest chance he would get punished.

This made me quietly confident for my quarter-final against Terry Griffiths, even though he'd had a good record against me earlier in the season. Terry is a very tough competitor whose safety and tactical play is among the best. I had played well against him in the World Matchplay at Brentwood, but lost 9–8 after leading 4–0; and in the Regal Scottish Masters at Motherwell he had beaten me 6–3. Another defeat came in the Benson & Hedges Masters at Wembley, Terry winning 5–2 for a place in the semi-finals. The only time I had got the better of him that season was in the Humo Belgian Masters in Antwerp.

Terry is a regular quarter-finalist in the Embassy World Championship: 1991 was the eighth successive year he had reached this stage of the tournament. That's a phenomenal record, and I knew I had a job on my hands to beat him.

This was amply proved in the match, when Terry cleared up four or five times to win frames in which I had led by 50 or so points. It was rather like a re-run of the World Matchplay, when he had done exactly the same to me.

At the Crucible I was leading 5–1, but Terry pegged me back to 7–7. I realized then that I had to tighten up my game a notch or two. I still felt pretty good because I knew I was doing my own stuff, which is half the battle, and I went on to lead 9–7 overnight. In the last frame of that session I made probably the best century of my life, a 101. I don't think I was in a single good position from start to finish of this break, but I kept it going to deny Terry any chance of pegging me back to 8–8.

Next day was a tense time for both of us. We were sweating blood to carve out even the smallest chances – but whenever they came it was pretty evil for whoever was on the receiving end. I extended my lead to three, only for Terry to close the gap to one at 11–10, clearing up as far as the pink in the 21st frame with a break of 52 – his fifth half century. However, I finished the match with breaks of 78 and 81 to complete two frames of snooker I'm very proud of. I remember them vividly. I dug in, saying to myself, 'Right, you know where you are going out there. Stick with it!' But it was a tremendous snooker match, and this was to prove the closest any player got to me at Sheffield. Terry had played exceptionally well: steady, relentless match-play. He doesn't do anything stupid and makes few unforced errors. You certainly have to earn your corn with him.

When I returned to the Grosvenor after the match, I still didn't know for sure who I would be playing in the semi-finals; it would be either Steve Davis or Dennis Taylor. I turned on the TV in my room to find the latest score on Teletext. I was hoping my opponent would be Dennis because I've had a consistently good record against him over the years. On the other hand you wouldn't want to bet against Steve beating him. In the event Steve won comfortably.

So here I was, playing him in the semi-finals after taking some good drubbings from him in the past – not least in the 1989 final here at the Crucible. Obviously this was going to be another tough match; but I was playing so well that I knew I had a golden opportunity to settle these old scores. Many people had been saying I wouldn't beat Davis, and one of the racing papers said he was my bogy man and that I couldn't possibly win.

I kept my own counsel and wasn't dismayed when I lost the first frame, which incidentally lasted 35 minutes and was the longest of the semi-final. You know that when you play Steve you are going to have to sweat it out. It's not just a matter of technique; you've got to be mentally tough and strategically at the top of your game. And if he is on form – as he usually is at the Crucible – and you beat him over the best of 31 frames, you are playing good snooker.

I knew I had hurt him when I took a 2–1 lead by winning the second frame on the black and the third on a re-spotted black. It was a wonderful fluke which enabled me to win the third frame, and from that moment I felt I was going to have a good match.

I'm not whingeing when I claim I've never really had a good run of the balls in all the years I've played Steve.

I think I failed because I was never totally confident of beating him – and when you are in that state of mind, Lady Luck has a nasty habit of deserting you. And, of course, the opposite is true too: when you're playing well, all the flukes go your way. Steve, hardened champion that he is, has always been horribly good at exploiting his opponents' errors to the maximum.

And so when, at the end of the third frame, that black doubled off two cushions and dropped in to take me 2–1 ahead, I said to myself: 'Right – this could be your time now.' After all, nothing like that had ever happened to me in all the matches I had played against him. I had attempted to double the black into the yellow pocket, but I misjudged the angle and it doubled back up the table and ambled into the top right-hand pocket.

As I went back to my chair I actually saw a flicker in Steve's face. It was plain that shot had hurt him. I thought at that moment that this could be the big turning point.

At the end of the first session I was leading 5–2; and my best break was an 80 in frame five. I was pretty elated, I can tell you. What I had to do now was prepare myself mentally for the next session and the predictable Davis rush – Steve's capacity to quicken the pace to get himself out of trouble. Surprisingly, on this occasion, however, he seemed unable to increase the momentum. I was now playing very steadily, doing nothing spectacular apart from compiling a break of 122 to lead 9–2. It was just good, hard snooker.

Steve now reverted to a much more tactical game, and I was forced to do the same to keep him at bay. In hindsight it's clear that this was the phase in which the match was won and lost: while Steve won eight of the last 15 frames, my seven were enough to win me a place in the final.

I kept Steve at arm's length by never letting him close the gap to less than four at 11–7, 12–8 and 14–10. But there was an evening session in the middle of the match which was one of the best I have ever played in since I first picked up a cue. Steve had thrown everything at me but I came out of the session 4–4 for a lead of 14–8. I couldn't have been more pleased if I had won a million pounds. To have been involved in a session like that and to have shared the eight frames when he had played so well helped me to sleep very, very contentedly that night. Steve must have been bitterly disappointed that he hadn't taken the session 5–3 or 6–2, which is what he needed to at that point. My pleasure lay chiefly in the fact that I was beating him with the same brand of ruthless tactical play with which he had become accustomed to crushing his opponents.

The next day I was able to carry on in the same vein and won 16–10, finishing the match with breaks of 86 and 64 in the last two frames – in which Steve never potted a ball.

As in my tough battle against Terry Griffiths in the previous round, I found I was able to step up a gear and finish the match.

Apart from being a great player, Steve is a true sportsman. But it was an unexpectedly fine gesture on his part to applaud me off the table at the end of the semi-final. I had never seen him do this before. As for my own feelings, it was a great relief to have beaten him in his own 'front room' at last. As I remarked at

Sheffield, over the years Steve has got to this stage of the World Championship so often he should be allowed to wear carpet slippers at the Crucible.

When I returned to the dressing room, I felt that my nightmare of losing 18–3 in the 1989 final was at last laid to rest.

My semi-final had finished first so I had to wait a few hours before knowing whether I would be playing Jimmy White or Steve James in the final. I fancied Jimmy to win, not because he was that far ahead as a player but because he had been in the final the year before as well as in 1984 and so had that little bit more experience. So it proved, Jimmy winning 16–9. Having to play Jimmy was a bit like Liverpool playing at Arsenal. I knew most of the crowd were going to be on Jimmy's side: he's lightning fast, plays brilliant and often thrillingly risky snooker, and is a character in himself.

I had a pretty sleepless night before the final. I don't drink much normally – just the occasional glass of wine with a meal – but I raided the mini-bar in my hotel room for a couple of cans of lager in the hope they would make me a bit drowsy. No luck, though. Next morning I relaxed as best as I could, watching a bit of television and attempting to do one of the Sunday newspaper crosswords.

As the time approached to leave the hotel, however, everything began to buzz. After all, this was the game I was waiting for. I just wanted to get out there and do the business.

I entered the Crucible via the stage door (the normal entrance for the players), signed a few autographs on the steps where quite a few fans had gathered, and soon was getting ready for the first session of the 35-frame final.

There were no thoughts in my mind of what happened in 1989. I had never felt so confident about a match in my life. I didn't think I was going to lose, but it was important that I got off to a good start in order to keep Jimmy's enthusiastic supporters quiet. I came down those steep steps into the arena absolutely charged up. I can't remember a single face in the audience, or even what the referee looked like. All I was aware of were the balls on the table, I was so locked into the game.

I made exactly the sort of start I wanted, winning the first frame in just nine minutes with a break of 97 to lead 1–0. I was very fluent, though I missed the last but one red with a century there for the taking. (I didn't know at the time that I was chasing the record number of eight century breaks in the World Championship, a figure Steve Davis set in 1986. I missed one on 97 in that first frame, another on 75 in the next, and eventually finished up equalling the record.)

It was great to get off to a flyer. It really put me on my game, and in the space of 73 minutes I built up a 7–0 lead with the help of further breaks of 88, 74 and (in the last frame of the session) 117.

I had scored exceptionally well: I had breaks of 39 and 43 in one of the two other frames and followed it with a 44. Considering the circumstances, I was playing the best snooker of my life. It was the culmination of all I had been doing for weeks in the practice room.

Then, back in my hotel room I started thinking about my 7–0 lead. I had the television on, and David Vine, discussing the first session, started telling everyone that both Eddie Charlton and Steve Davis had led by seven frames in the final but finished up losing. I switched over to another channel. I had no intention of flooding my mind with negative thoughts. My view was that I was playing to such a high standard that all I had to do was nurse the lead I had built up. I wasn't going to try anything spectacular in the two middle sessions, but I wanted to be sure of snapping up every chance Jimmy gave me as well as carving out my own opportunities.

I was fully aware Jimmy was going to have a go and try to get back at me. As it turned out, there were three frames in the match which I think were vital. One was the 16th, the last of the first day's play, which I won with a break of 112 to lead 11–5 overnight. The others were frames 19 and 21, both of which I won on the black to go ahead 12–7 and 13–8. I was in fact getting pretty good with the counter-punch. Every time Jimmy started to come back, I hit him with a century or a very timely clearance. This can eventually become demoralizing – and I know what I'm talking about because I've been on the receiving end myself.

To lead 11–5 was very satisfying, but I couldn't sleep at all that night, and ended up with the white sheet over my head on top of the pillow. I don't know how it got there, and I probably drove Karen absolutely mad. But I was so wound up that, although sleepless, I was relieved when morning came.

My first thoughts next day were pretty negative. Although I had a six-frame lead, all I could think about was the formidable task of having to win another seven.

106

But gradually I got things into perspective. After all, Jimmy had to win 13 out of the remaining 19 frames, so how must he be feeling?

When the final resumed, Jimmy won three of the first four frames. But, as I said, the 19th frame (the third of that quartet) was a crucial one. I nicked it 51–50 with a clearance of 34 – straightforward enough, though under the circumstances a very tense affair.

The next frame Jimmy closed to 12–8, and many of his supporters will think he should have made it 12–9. But when he was 55–40 he missed the blue with the rest; normally you would have expected him to get it. Then I nicked the blue in, potted the pink, and finally took the frame with a cracking black off the cushion.

When I knocked the black in to lead 13–8, I knew that was it – the killer blow – because Jimmy was fully aware he should have won that frame. These sudden, unexpected setbacks really hurt – I knew, I'd been having them from Steve Davis for years.

I finished off that session with breaks of 52 and 34 to lead 15–9, and began the last session with a break of 112, my eighth century of the championship. I went on to within one frame of victory at 17–10; but I was still on edge as Jimmy pulled back another one. There was no way I would be able to relax until the match was over, but Jimmy let me in for what proved to be the last time when, attempting a safety shot, he saw the cue ball strike the knuckle of a middle pocket. A break of 48 followed and now there was no way back for him. Shortly afterwards Jimmy conceded – and there I was, 'Champion of the World'!

Looking back, I think the greatest statistical com-

pliment on my performance is that none of my
opponents was able to finish within three frames of me.

I could sympathize with Jimmy: three finals, three
defeats. He too has had to bear the bridesmaid tag. He's
unquestionably the best player never (so far!) to have
won the World Championship. But he'll be back again,
giving it his best shot. There's also his dad Tom, who
I've got to know quite well over the years. Jimmy has
had plenty of successes, and he beat me in the World
Matchplay final. But this was the title Tom wanted for
'my Jim', as he calls him. Against any other player I,
too, would probably have been rooting for 'my Jim'.

As for our celebrations, we didn't go mad or jump
into any fountains in the city. A few drinks, yes – but
basically it was an occasion to relish quietly with my
wife and family, Phil, his wife Jean, and Tony, and
Karen's parents. I had no idea my parents and stepfather would be at the final. I had phoned my father in
the afternoon, but nothing had been said about that –
which made it all the more of a surprise when I saw
everyone afterwards. Needless to say, Phil had
arranged it all.

Karen greeted me just after the trophy had been
presented. She is a bit shy and it wasn't until I caught
her eye back-stage that she came out to face the
cameras. I know quite a few players and managers
think that wives shouldn't be at events as important
as this until the very end. Well, that may suit some
people, but Karen is not just my wife – she is my best
friend and understands me better than anyone else.
Her presence at these events is a terrific source of
strength because I can talk through all my worries

with her. I think this is a reflection of the fact that I'm basically a home person anyway. I'm not the greatest lover of hotels, so the more my environment away from the snooker table resembles home, the better I'm likely to play. Phil, who knows me pretty well by now, is completely sympathetic to my feelings on this matter. And my winning the World Championship in the presence of Karen, Phil and Tony proved that the Parrott 'team' has got a lot going for it.

14

Life at the Top

Since winning the World Championship I have had to
face up to a fairly heavy schedule, though I did manage
to get away with Karen for a holiday in the Caribbean.

I received hundreds of letters, and for a week or so
it was almost a full time job just to open them. A friend
also sent me a cutting from the *Daily Telegraph* in
which a picture showed 'Steve Parrott after winning
the Embassy World Championship.' I think there are
enough 'Steves' and 'Stephens' at the top already.

Being a world champion has meant far more local
recognition than I've ever had before. These days I
can't go into Liverpool city centre without being recognized. I've tried the incognito approach, wearing a
track suit and training shoes, but I'm still spotted. On
one occasion, though, a shop assistant in WH Smith's
didn't believe it was me when I bought two copies of
the June edition of *Snooker Scene*, which contained
full reports of my Embassy World Championship
victory. On the cover was a picture of me holding the
world trophy. The assistant looked at it, glanced up in
my direction, then shrugged her shoulders, as if to say,
'No, that can't be him.'

Perhaps the most pleasant occasion of all was to be given a civic reception by the Lord Mayor of Liverpool, Trevor Smith. To be honoured in this way was a very nice gesture, particularly when you bear in mind the torrid time the council was going through in May 1991. Representatives of all political parties were at the reception and I was able to chat at length to the Lord Mayor about my world victory. Karen was with me, and the Parrott party also included my Mum, Dad and stepfather, Karen's family, Phil and his wife and family, and Tony and his wife. It was a very interesting and enjoyable evening which lasted something like three hours, and after a superb dinner the usual photographs were taken to mark the occasion.

I had to turn down at least three invitations to visit Chester races on Cup day, to my great regret. The Roodeye is one of my favourite tracks, and the May meeting always attracts several very useful horses. John McCririck, that champion tipster from Channel 4's racing team, was among those who had invited me to Chester but I had so many television, radio and business commitments it was impossible to find the time to go.

In fact it wasn't until four weeks after winning the championship that I was able to start winding down. I did manage to see the Derby at Epsom. Karen and I were guests of an international company, with whom we had dinner and a glass or two of wine. John McCririck interviewed me during Channel 4's outside broadcast, and I also took on an assignment for BBC Radio 5 throughout the afternoon. This simply involved general chit-chat about snooker. I did three or four interviews and at the end of each one gave my selection for the next race. Would you believe it? With millions listening in, the world snooker champion and horse-fancier couldn't find a single winner.

By the time I returned to our hospitality suite after one interview it was too late to back anything as the next race had already started. Imagine my chagrin when I found that a friend in the know had left a message advising me to back Sylva Honda – which did the business at 20–1!

It was still a super day at Epsom. I love going racing, I think it must be in my blood, and to go to the Derby and combine it with just a little work was so enjoyable.

I've been a racing fan for as long as I can remember. My dad has always liked a little bet. I suppose that, seeing the morning newspaper open at the racing page for so many years, it was natural for me to take an interest as well. Another fan is Jimmy White's dad Tom, who is never without a copy of the *Sporting Life* in his overcoat pocket.

One day perhaps I will own a racehorse myself. It's an ambition of mine but not just yet. I just couldn't give it enough time. I have a couple of good trainer friends who I'm quite pally with. One of them is Mike O'Neill who I have known for a good few years – he trains about 20 minutes from where I live. He is doing really well and I have had invitations to go to his yard, have breakfast with him and see the horses working. To me that would be a terrific day out. Mike, of course, had the fabulous experience of winning the Gold Cup at Ayr at 50 to 1 in his first year as a trainer.

The most coveted trophy in snooker, and a very proud moment
for me.

A special moment with the 'Parrott team': Phil, Karen and Tony.

'A word from our sponsors' ... celebrating with Peter Middleton
and Peter Dyke from Imperial Tobacco.

With the Lord Mayor of Liverpool, Trevor Smith, and Karen at the civic reception held in my honour, June 1991. (*Liverpool Daily Post and Echo*)

The WPBSA Golf Day at St Pierre, Chepstow, in May 1991. At this annual event snooker players, friends and guests get together to raise money to provide powered wheelchairs for handicapped youngsters.

One of the proudest moments . . . At Anfield with the trophy before
the last home game of the season against Spurs, 11 May 1991.

I've actually ridden a horse myself and while I'm much too overweight for racing there is another problem, I'm useless, so I have no aspirations at all of ever trying to race one. I'll leave all that to Graham Bradley, a jockey friend of mine who I met for the first time at one of our local racecourses.

Graham is a keen snooker player. He's been to my house and I've given him a few lessons. I've watched him racing over the jumps and consider him to be among the top three pilots in the country. It's nice to see he's getting a lot more mounts again because I think he is a very talented rider. If I did become an owner it would be my ambition to win the Champion Hurdle. I prefer the spectacle of National Hunt racing to the flat, and hurdle races rather than steeplechases. Every season I keep tabs on the juvenile hurdlers in the hope that I can spot the one that will win the Champion later. My ultimate aim is, one day, to buy a good mile-and-a-half flat-racing horse with a view to winning the Champion with it.

Another sporting interest of mine is golf though sadly these days I'm not able to play as much as I would like to. My home club is West Derby and my handicap is seven (though heaven knows if I could play to it at present, when I have hardly any time to practise). Originally I had a handicap of 14, but because I won a couple of club tournaments I had to volunteer to be docked. So my handicap was cut to nine – and after I won another event it was cut to seven. In those days I was playing twice a day and getting in 36 holes. In 1987 the club championship was won with two rounds of 74, if my memory is correct; and I shot a 73 and 74 in the colts to win the age group with a better aggregate score.

Some years ago, when I was playing a lot of golf, it was often on some of our fine local courses with my friends Dave Atherton, his son Graham, and Jimmy Bush. Dave and Jimmy are also two of my most fervent supporters, and over the years came to hundreds of matches, together with their wives Joyce and Margaret. Not just fair-weather friends, they came along even when I was going through bad spells – and there were plenty of those!

Dave, Joyce and Graham were at the Crucible this year as usual, and it was a special pleasure to be able to invite them to the reception which is held at the Grosvenor Hotel each year after the final has been won. As always, the Embassy people laid on a magnificent spread.

I don't get much time to play golf these days and, sadly, I don't have nearly as much time as I would like to see old and new friends. But I'll always remember the support and encouragement I received from Dave, Joyce, Graham, Jimmy and Margaret.

One event I was delighted to take part in was the WPBSA's golf day which has been held at that lovely championship course of St Pierre, Chepstow, for the past two years. No prizes this time. But our annual golf day is a special occasion for the players as it is held for the sole purpose of raising funds for the provision of powered wheelchairs for handicapped youngsters. We've already managed to finance more than a hundred. To see the happy faces of the youngsters (and their parents) as they receive their wheelchairs makes the occasion such a worthwhile exercise for all concerned. Another golf charity day I was involved in concerned the Sunshine Variety Club and their annual Northern tournament which was held at Wallasey Golf Club. Again, a very worthwhile cause which I was only too happy to support.

15

Player Tales

The snooker circuit often buzzes with rumour, gossip, and anecdotes about the players. I've heard of and directly witnessed a good few myself over the years, and if I recall some of them here I hope no one is going to be too offended.

Steve James is involved in several of the more recent stories, and I heard this priceless exchange after he had beaten Stephen Hendry to reach the semi-finals of the 1991 World Championship at the Crucible. Steve Rider was speaking to Jamesy backstage at the Crucible during a live link-up with the *Sportsnight* studios in London. I saw the link-up on the television set in my room at the Grosvenor, and fell off the bed laughing when the interview finished more or less as follows:

Rider: 'Well Steve, it's a one-table situation for the semi-finals. Do you think this might be a little strange for you?'

Jamesy: 'No, of course not. I played in the final of the Mercantile Credit Classic last year, and I think that was one-table as well.'

That, for those who know him, is a classic Jamesy line. He often comes out with 'funnies' without immediately realizing what he's said. His deadpan West Midland accent only serves to make it sound even funnier.

A Belgian journalist could see the funny side when she asked Steve during the championship if he had played much in Belgium. 'Stacks of times,' said Jamesy. 'Oh, whereabouts?' she enquired. James looked blank for a moment, then yelled at his manager: 'Ramsey, where have I played in Belgium?'

One day last season Steve was telling all and sundry he'd been nicked for speeding in his BMW. He concluded wryly: 'It's a pity I wasn't riding me bike – the cops wouldn't have caught me on that.'

(Apparently 'me bike' is his 750cc Honda RC30, which he claims is capable of about 180 mph. On sober reflection, I don't think I'll ride pillion with him.)

One of my favourite tales about Jimmy White concerns the trip we made to Australia to play in the 1985 Winfield Masters. It was a horrendous journey which took more than 30 hours. It was about 1 o'clock in the afternoon when we were transferred from the airport to the Hilton Hotel in Sydney. There were about 10 of us, including Jimmy, John Virgo, Alex Higgins, Willie Thorne, Joe Johnson and Tony Meo (who won the event).

Most of us got changed straight away, and after a wash and brush up we headed for the City Tatts, a snooker club across the road where we were allowed to practise. I decided to have a cup of tea and a sandwich before loosening up at the practice table. Jimmy, who looked as if he had just rolled out of a hedge backwards, was first to get his cue out of the case, and at this Bill

Werberniuk asked him if he wanted a game. Bill had been in Australia for three or four days, had acclimatized to the conditions and had put in a fair amount of practice at the club. He obviously felt his chances of beating Jimmy were pretty good, so he suggested they play for a pound a point. As 'Our Jim' can never resist this sort of invitation the scene was set for some fun and games.

The first frame saw Bill break off – only for Jimmy to go to the table and compile a maximum break of 147. Bearing in mind that Jimmy hadn't even had a practice shot since leaving England and looked as if he could sleep for a week, it was a pretty staggering performance. Poor old Bill couldn't believe it. But he decided to try and get some money back by playing another frame, only to be brushed aside again by the whirlwind, who this time fattened the coffers with a break of 106. Bill now put his cue away and retired gracefully from the scene after settling his debts. I bet he's never lost money as quick as that before.

Another of my favourite stories concerning Jimmy involved his dad Tom. They were in the departure lounge at Heathrow waiting to board a flight to Canada. Suddenly Tom turned to Jimmy and said: 'Look, son – there's Vera Lynn.' Jim admits he turned 20 shades of pale when Tom said to him, 'I haven't spoken to Vera for years, I'm going over to see how she is.'

Well, Jimmy thought this was a lousy idea, even if his dad *was* one of Vera Lynn's oldest fans. It was all likely to end in embarrassment, he thought, and urged his father to forget about it. But Tom would have none of that. He walked over to the singer and said, 'Hello Vera, how are you?'

Jimmy feared the worst, but to his amazement Vera greeted his dad like a long-lost friend. He could hardly believe it particularly when Tom told him later that Vera had sung at Tooting Hippodrome when he worked there over 40 years before. They hadn't seen each other since then, but she recognized him all the same.

Willie Thorne is one of the wittiest players on the circuit. Stephen Hendry, in fact, insists Willie is the funniest man he has ever met. It's not that he tells jokes: his speciality is the deadpan one-liner, the drier the better.

One day during a tournament in New Zealand we were invited onto a luxury cabin cruiser, which we were told had cost £300,000. I remember the day very well, the sun was shining, it was very warm and we were being taken to a beach for a barbecue. Most of the players taking part in the event, Stephen Hendry and Mike Hallett among them, were also on board. As we lounged around on the upper deck Willie, who was nattily dressed for the occasion in shorts, summer shirt, sunhat and beach shoes, looked about him and drawled: 'I wonder what the rich people are doing today.'

While in New Zealand Willie, Stephen, Mike and Dennis Taylor took in a round of golf during another free day. All went well until they came to the last hole, which proved to be quite a test for them as their tee shots had to be fired through a narrow gap between hedges and trees.

Mike, Stephen and Dennis safely found the fairway. Then it was Willie's turn. As he practised his swing and lined up his tee shot, you could hear a pin drop.

Slowly, Willie began his backswing. Then, just as he reached the top of the backswing, a bird in a nearby bush burst into song.

'Tweet! Tweet!' went the birdie. 'Bloody Hell!' went Willie. 'Crash!' went the ball, as it carved its way into the nearest shrubbery. His playing partners collapsed into helpless laughter. At last Willie regained his composure, looked in the direction of his feathered heckler, and said quietly: 'Nice bird, nice bird. Until I came along, I bet that's never happened here.'

Willie and Stephen love to put one over each other. At the 1989 Embassy World Championship it was the 'the Great WT's' turn to get in the first dig. Stephen was practising on the table close to the television studio when Willie, immaculate in his Sunday best, walked in with his cue and case.

The two of them were due to meet in the second round later that day and Willie, after removing his cue from the case, took his coat off and got down to play a long red, which flew into a top pocket. At this he stood up, placed his cue back in the case and put his coat on. Stephen, wearing his practice outfit of jeans and T-shirt, looked somewhat bemused and asked: 'Aren't you going to practise, Willie?'

At the door of the practice room, Willie turned, gazed levelly at Stephen and replied: 'I don't need to for you, son.' First points to Willie – but game, set and match to Stephen, who walloped his friend 13–4.

I think the best example of Willie's wit at its driest also came in the World Championship. Stephen was playing exceptionally well and potting everything in sight. At one point he was left an easy opportunity with the red over the pocket. Willie was standing there, holding his cue and watching. Stephen decided to play a very attacking shot and smash the reds up, trusting to luck a little that the cue ball would finish in a reasonable position. Anyway, he sank the red and the cue ball smashed the reds all over the place. The white then cannoned the pink, promoting it towards the middle pocket. Finally, when all the balls came to rest, by some outrageous miracle a gap had appeared through a forest of reds, allowing an easy pink into the middle pocket.

Willie, not a flicker of expression passing over his face, murmured 'Unlucky!' – and sat down. Stephen couldn't control himself and burst into a fit of laughter.

Eddie Charlton is another player who's the subject of a good many stories. During the 1990 European Open at Lyon, a few of us were sitting in the balcony area watching Eddie's match against Doug Mountjoy drag to a conclusion – the other three games that had begun at the same time had finished long ago. My wife Karen looked up at the scoreboard and, turning to me, asked: 'What does the A.M. after Eddie's name stand for?'

Quick as a flash I replied: 'That's when he usually finishes, love.' I couldn't resist that one. Besides, Eddie's a real character who doesn't mind a quip or two at his expense.

Earlier in 1990 the Asian Open ranking tournament was played to a finish in the Chinese city of Guangzhou. Now getting into or out of China involves interminable delays at customs; but after surviving checkpoint after checkpoint, we were nearly all through. I turned round to look behind, and there was Eddie, miles away from us at the back of the queue. Terry Smith, the editor of *Pot Black*, was standing next to me and I said to him, 'Look at that, Terry – Eddie's taking the longest to queue up as usual'.

He may be a bit slow at the table, but Eddie would whip the pants off a lot of his fellow professionals when it comes to fitness. During the 1989 Hong Kong Open he was among a group of players who went out on a cruise just off the mainland. We moored in the bay so that those of us who wanted to could have a swim. Eddie stripped down to his swimming trunks, dived overboard – and headed for the nearest beach, which was about a mile away. Once there, he ran for as far as the eye could see before diving into the sea and swimming back to us. When he climbed back on to the boat, Eddie smiled and remarked in his Aussie drawl: 'Right, I'm ready for my chicken now.'

What an incredible man! He's been a boxer, a surfer, has played soccer, has carried the Olympic torch, and has played and beaten the best snooker players in the world. He's flown more than a million miles and has made over 100 trips from Australia to England and back. A special medal should be struck just for him.

John Spencer is perhaps the biggest wind-up artist on the snooker circuit, and not even the BBC's executive producer for snooker, Nick Hunter, was immune to a Spencer Special when news leaked out three years ago that he was to be promoted to Assistant Head of the Sport and Events Group in London. Nick had been part of the snooker scene since 1977, and to mark his contribution to the game he was summoned to the

WPBSA hospitality room at the Crucible for a small presentation and thank-you ceremony.

The room was packed out for the presentation when Spenny, who had organized everything, entered bearing a tray full of crystal glasses. Turning to Nick, Spenny told him that the gift was from the WPBSA and a few friends. But just as he was about to hand Nick the tray, Spenny tripped and the whole lot went crashing to the floor, sending splinters of glass all over the place. Nick looked absolutely aghast.

Spenny picked himself up and said: 'Well, it's a good job that wasn't the real lot.' When the uproar had died down, Spenny produced the real gift from behind a curtain. It emerged that he'd spent a few quid buying some cheap glasses from the local market that morning.

Steve Davis, of course, is Mr Cool personified. Millions of TV viewers have marvelled at the icy calm he displays at the snooker table, but for me the most striking example of his legendary composure occurred during a flight home from Hong Kong, where I had taken part in one of Barry Hearn's invitation events, the 1988 LEP Hong Kong Masters. I was sitting next to Dennis Taylor, who had taken two sleeping tablets for the 14-hour straight-through flight home. Steve, a few seats away, had a blanket over his head, which was resting against a cushion. Then, without warning, we ran into turbulence and the airliner suddenly dropped several thousand feet towards earth. Sleeping tablets or no, Dennis was wide awake in two seconds flat, demanding to know what the hell was going on. Even veteran traveller Barry turned more than a trifle pale. Steve? He might just as well have been in his favourite armchair at home. His head stayed on the cushion; the blanket was undisturbed....

My first overseas trips came during my amateur career, when I accompanied first Joe Johnson and later Neal Foulds to Zimbabwe. Joe, who was by now a professional, was great company. He loves a sing-song, (he often performs in public) and led the singing when we wound down each evening.

Outside the main cities in Zimbabwe the equipment at the clubs often leaves something to be desired. At one I went to with Joe, we were told: 'We knew you were coming, so we sent the table to the butcher to have the pockets cut correctly.' Apparently the butcher was the only person who had a sharp enough knife for this work. When he finished he stapled the cloth to the side of the pocket. You could actually see the staples jutting out. Joe was still able to make a break of 54, which would have been worth a century anywhere else. If the ball landed near a cushion it was a waste of time: there was no way you could pot it.

A few years later, just after Karen and I were married, we were in New Zealand and one evening went out for dinner at a nice restaurant. Joe was a member of the party, and he gave a beautiful rendition of 'Ave Maria' in our honour. He really is one of the nicest men you could ever want to meet.

And finally....A few years ago John Virgo, Jimmy White, Tony Meo and I were in the transit lounge at Bahrain airport en route to Australia. John was quietly licking an ice cream when this gentleman in Arab costume and sun glasses came up, snatched the ice cream from him, and started eating it himself. JV was flabbergasted. It must have been fully half a minute before he realized that the Eastern gent was none other than Alex Higgins, who had bought the costume in Dubai, where he had been playing some private exhibitions. His duties over in the Gulf, Alex had then flown to Bahrain to catch up with the jumbo taking the rest of us 'down under'.

16

Old Contemporaries

I'm often asked the age-old question: Who is or was the best player the game has ever seen?

I know two people – one of them a player, the other a BBC commentator – who are absolutely sure they know the answer. For Fred Davis and Ted Lowe, Joe Davis is the No. 1. Ted and Fred's choice will have plenty of support, but I'm not competent to offer an opinion. I never saw Joe play: he retired some years before I was even born. But his record alone proves that Joe must have been one helluva player. Dad swore by the Joe Davis method when he coached me as a youngster, and Joe's books are still in perfect condition at his home.

Joe was the undefeated world champion from 1927 until his retirement from the championship in 1946. He was unbeaten in 34 world championship matches – a quite remarkable record. It must not be forgotten that Joe had no one to coach or teach him how to play snooker. He had to learn everything on his own, and many of today's shots were invented by him.

I have seen a video of Joe making a hundred break, and from that alone you can see he is a class player who must be given a very high rating on the list of all-time greats. There wasn't the competition around in Joe's days – there weren't as many world-class players as today's snooker stars have to face – but there's no doubt he would have been exceptional in whatever era he played.

Dad saw Joe play at the St George's Hall in Liverpool. It was rather mundane snooker during the afternoon session, in which Joe shared the eight frames played. The story goes that Joe collared the table fitter between sessions and told him to check the table thoroughly with a spirit level as the playing surface was untrue. Joe left in a huff for a bite to eat, but he returned in the evening to play some immaculate snooker which included a couple of century breaks. Before leaving for his hotel, he made a point of commending the fitter for his work on the table. Unknown to Joe, however, the fitter had done precisely nothing. He had simply taken his tools out of the box while Joe was there and put them away again when he left. There was nothing wrong with the table anyway; it was spot on.

As for Fred Davis, I only caught the tail end of his better years, and even then he was over 60. At the outset I didn't think Fred had a good cue action; it was short and more suited to billiards. But of course his game developed in an era when the top players were masters at both games. In those days power cue actions didn't figure quite so much in snooker. But Fred had a tremendous touch around the black spot, and of course he was as wily as an old fox.

He is definitely from the old school. Just the mention

of his name conjures up his infectious smile and the familiar 'Er, um ...' which usually precedes anything he has to say. He isn't doing so well these days, but if I'm still playing snooker at the age of 78, I'll be happy.

John Pulman is another of the 'golden oldies' I saw little of as a player. But I vividly recall that time he missed a red (or was it the yellow?) during his 1977 Embassy World Championship semi-final against John Spencer. You didn't need to be a lip reader to know what John muttered in front of the camera as he went back to his chair.

'Pully' is a real character. One of the best nights I had on the circuit was one I spent with John, Dennis Taylor and Rex Williams. They were working their way steadily through a bottle of whisky, and after Rex poured me a drink, I sat and listened as 'Pully' recalled the time he went to play an exhibition in Ipswich. He turned up immaculately dressed: his hair was greased back, and he wore a long mohair coat over his dress suit. He was of course holding his cue and case in his hand. After knocking on the door, 'Pully' walked in and was confronted by the club steward, who smiled at him. 'Ah, you must be the snooker player then?' 'Pully', in that sarcastic way of his, replied, 'No, I'm the f ... chimney sweep!' He was never invited back. And when Dennis played there some time later, 'Pully' was referred to as a 'very ignorant man'.

Pully was a very tough competitor – his record of eight World Championships is testimony to that. 'How can you fail with initials like J.P.?' he always says to me.

Rex Williams is out of the same school as Pulman,

and I have a lot of time for him. He tells the story of when he went to play an exhibition at an outpost somewhere in the jungle in Africa. For the final leg of the journey he had to cross a crocodile-infested lake in a large, crudely built canoe. Rex must have been a fine sight in his dress suit and topcoat. A young black was on the oar, while the pipe-smoking skipper stood at the back admiring the scenery. They were only half way across the lake when the skipper stumbled and his pipe dropped into the water. When they had made it to the other side and Rex had disembarked, the oarsman was ordered to go back and find the pipe. By some miracle he recovered the pipe after an underwater search. How he managed to find it before becoming a tasty morsel for the crocs remained a mystery.

I never played against Rex on the professional circuit. While he was still doing quite well in the latter part of the 1980s, I don't think he now has quite the dedication he had in the old days.

He has unquestionably been a great player, even though a major snooker title eluded him. His safety play was exceptional, and I have a lot of respect for a player who won both the World and the UK billiards championship earlier in his career.

17

Friends, Rivals & Others

RAY REARDON

Of all the many letters I have received since winning the Embassy World Championship, one means more to me than any of the others. In fact, I've had the letter framed and it's now prominently displayed in the snooker room at home. It is from six-times world champion Ray Reardon. It is short, but every word counts: 'Congratulations John, I couldn't be more pleased.' The letter, on Ray's personal writing paper, was a wonderful gesture and absolutely typical of the man.

I became a Ray Reardon fan the first time I saw him play, on television many years ago. He has always struck me as the perfect embodiment of how the game should be played. I have always preferred to watch the complete players in action. Ray was one of them. In the 1970s he was the boss – a superb all-round player, whose tactical acumen has been bettered in my time only by Steve Davis at his very best.

Right from the beginning of our association Phil advised me to watch Ray whenever possible. We used to call him the 'archangel of clear-ups' because he was so deadly if you let him in with four or five reds left on the table and the frame still wide open.

I remember watching Ray in the 1974 world final against Graham Miles. He won the match 22–12 and must have come through and won at least 10 of those frames after being 40 or 50 points behind. Then there was an exhibition at The Cherry Tree in St Helens. Ray was fantastic that evening and made three century breaks: he was simply in a different class.

Even as he walked on to the stage to take part in Jim Davidson's television show *Big Break*, Ray – now many years past his prime – looked every inch a multiple champion. He was totally professional in his manner and immaculately turned out. You knew from the moment you saw him that he had been the business. The man has an aura.

I once played Ray when someone sitting near the front row rustled something which I took to be a bag of crisps. Ray didn't say anything; he simply gave the offender a laser-beam look. I half expected the victim to disappear in a puff of smoke. There was also an occasion when Ray was about to play a shot at the precise moment when a spectator walked to his seat carrying a pint of beer in either hand and some wrapped pies held by the arms against his chest. Ray stood up and after slowly shaking his head in that characteristic way, asked: 'Would you like some sauce for that lot?'

When Ray played Roy Connor one year in the upstairs snooker room at Pontin's holiday camp in Prestatyn, he had to give him 25 points start. At the time Roy was a very good amateur player and when he was drawn against Ray I know he fancied his chances

131

with a start like that on one of the less fashionable upstairs tables. As it turned out, Ray absolutely paralysed him to win 4–0. What Roy forgot is that Ray was brought up on tables like that. A lot of top players might have complained at the conditions. Ray just got on with the job in hand.

I played Ray only once in a ranking event – the 1985 Embassy World Championship. He beat me 13–12 in the quarter-finals. Even then he was still a hard and mean competitor, and after I led 9–7 he played the best snooker I had seen from him for five or six years. There was a school of thought that Ray, to use one expression I overheard, had by then 'gone at the game'. Well, in that match he displayed many of his old skills. As I remarked to some of the doubters, 'Anyone who thinks he's gone should go out there and try playing him.'

Ray's professional career did start to go back a season or so later, and it must have been very difficult for him, knowing how well he had performed in previous years. I was sad to hear that the 1991 Embassy was his last world-ranking tournament.

Ray has been a great player and a great ambassador for the game. He is someone I really respect, a professional through and through. He has his little mannerisms, his own ways and we will all miss him at the major events.

JOHN SPENCER

John Spencer and I have several things in common apart from winning the Embassy World Championship. Despite John's Manchester connections, we both played in and represented the Bootle Snooker League as amateurs, and the names of Spencer and Parrott can be found among the winners of the Merseyside individual championship; John won in 1965 and I 17 years later.

I made my first competitive century break playing for the Dudley Institute in the Bootle League. And a few years after completing his National Service in the Royal Air Force, John was persuaded to pop across to Merseyside from his Ratcliffe base to play for Wavertree Labour Club. That was a bit before my time, but a few years later I was to play at the Wavertree in League matches.

I often watched John play after I took up the game seriously. We met for the first time at the television studios in Manchester. John was chatting about snooker on a kid's afternoon TV show and I was the junior guest. I was about 14 at the time and we played a frame of snooker. John also did the 'line-up' to show the young viewers how to practise, and I remember he cleared the table. John asked me what my highest break was. I said, a little sheepishly, 'Only 51, Mr Spencer.' He replied, 'You should be able to do better than that, the way you cue. But keep at it, young man.'

In 1985 I played John in the first round of the Embassy World Championship and beat him 10–3. When I won the title six years later, John offered me some words of wisdom on the ways my victory would affect my life, and I will always be indebted to him for that.

I've always enjoyed watching John play. There's no doubt about it, he and Ray Reardon were two of the three biggest names in the game during the 1970s – the other player, of course, being Alex Higgins.

John used an Adam two-piece cue when he won the Embassy World Championship in 1977. He was the first player to capture the title using a two piece. It was made in Japan, which everyone thought was ridiculous; but if there are any still around today I doubt if they cost less than £100. They are very good cues, and I used a Spencer-endorsed model for a time.

I was at the Crucible Theatre in 1978 for the Embassy World Championship when John compiled a break of 138, the highest of the televised stages that year. It earned him the princely sum of £500. It was a magnificent effort and the break was afterwards shown repeatedly on television. There weren't many televised centuries in those days, and John's was one of only seven made at the Crucible that year.

John was a player of tremendous flair; he had great touch and was a pleasure to watch. He was also a lethal long potter, and his use of deep screw was quite incredible.

In recent years John has suffered from double vision – a disastrous complaint for any sportsman whose game depends on hand-eye coordination of a high order. Typically, John is never slow to make fun of his predicament. He once told me that whenever he sees two yellows, he always goes for the one that's easier to pot! It's difficult now for John to cue properly, and the double vision has often been accompanied by terrible headaches; thankfully these are nothing like as bad as they used to be.

Over the years John has been a very active participant and board member of the WPBSA. He is now the chairman and is doing a grand job at an important period in the sport's history. He is very much a player's chairman – which is just as it should be.

It could be argued that John's playing record, in spite of his three world titles, and victories in the very first Benson & Hedges Masters, the Wilson Classic (later the Lada Classic), the Winfield Australian Masters, and the Holsten Lager, doesn't fully reflect his ability. And it really wasn't his day when the television cameras failed to record a 147 break he made during the Holsten event at Slough in 1979. In fact it's a great loss to snooker fans generally that the crew were taking a meal break as John took the first three frames off Cliff Thorburn 106–0, 147–0 and 119–0. Over-generous pockets in the match table meant the break could not be ratified for record purposes. It's ironic that John was the other player when Steve Davis compiled the first official maximum during the 1982 Lada Classic.

ALEX HIGGINS

For all his idiosyncrasies and in spite of his troubles over the years, Alex deserves a lot of credit for keeping snooker in the public eye before the boom began at the start of the 1980s. Today's players owe Alex a great debt of gratitude for this.

I went to the Crucible in 1979 to watch Alex play Terry Griffiths in the Embassy World Championship quarter-finals. It was one of the greatest matches I have ever seen or am likely to see. When Alex performs like that he takes some stopping and Terry had to play out of his brains to win 13–12. It was tremendous entertainment.

Alex's talent seems to have waned slightly in recent seasons. His game has lost that razor-sharp edge – and, of course, off the table he has had a variety of personal problems which haven't helped him one bit. Alex just doesn't look after himself in the way that he should do. He is easily upset, has a very short fuse and can become very hot-headed indeed. I have been with Alex at exhibitions and I'd like to state that he gets far more hassle than anyone else I know. He is a magnet for nut cases, and if there are any of these around they quickly attach themselves to him.

Over the years I have played Alex quite a few times, though not very often in ranking tournaments, and so far he has beaten me only in an invitation event in Australia. It was held at the Anzac Memorial Club in Sydney and was one of Eddie Charlton's promotions. The matches were decided over the aggregate score of three frames, and I was virtually out of contention after Alex made a break of 135 in the second.

During another visit 'down under' we all took time off from playing in the Winfield Masters to go to the races at one of the Sydney tracks. Jockey Kevin Moses, a friend of Alex, told him to back a horse he was riding that afternoon. Everybody wanted to borrow money to get on, but Alex thought he knew better and put his money elsewhere. He went barmy when Kevin's horse came in at 20–1.

Alex came from the backstreets of Belfast – the district known as the Jampot – where he first picked up his cue. He's never had a coaching lesson in his life, which speaks volumes for his natural ability. That he could just go about it the way he has done and become a world champion is quite remarkable. His actual technique is not something that youngsters should copy, however, because he moves around a lot and jumps up off the shot (though by the time he does that he's got through the ball).

On his best days he has the priceless gift, when in trouble, of changing up a gear and winning two or three frames very quickly. What he should be better known for – and what even his toughest opponents acknowledge – is that when he needs to play safe he can make life extremely difficult for the opposition. He's a very good tactician when he wants to be – it just surprises me he has exploited this gift and displayed his all-round game so rarely.

At his best Alex is a phenomenal player. He is so hard to stop and can play unbelievable snooker. But it doesn't surprise me that he loses far more often than he should, because he's too inclined to play to the crowd – the self-styled 'People's Champion'.

He has probably kicked himself umpteen times for losing to Cliff Thorburn in the 1980 Embassy World Final and to Dennis Taylor in the final of the 1987 Benson & Hedges Masters. I couldn't see Steve Davis losing from the position Alex put himself in against Dennis at Wembley. But while Steve plays granite snooker for frame after frame, Alex attacks most of the time and that can be fatal.

Is Alex lucky to be back playing professional snooker after his season-long ban? Many believe his 12-month 'holiday' must be his last chance. You just can't keep doing the things he has done and expect to be allowed to continue playing. Alex has had plenty of slaps on the wrist, fines and suspensions over the years. If you go around punching or head butting officials, you can't expect your Association to want you to be involved in the game. Hopefully his latest and most severe ban will have given Alex time to think seriously about what he has done.

Phil and I gave Alex a lift home one night after we had played each other in the Matchroom League. On this occasion we were able to witness a much more laid-back attitude. Alex had recently broken a bone in his foot, and I recall how he was obliged to hop from shot to shot around the table. I won 7–1 that evening.

Alex was living at a place called Ramsbottom. He called it 'Sheepsass', which was something I didn't understand when I asked him where he wanted us to drive him. As soon as he sat down in the passenger seat of the car he was puffing away at the first of many cigarettes. I don't smoke and normally I wouldn't allow anyone to smoke in my car. But Alex was well alight and I thought, 'Oh, well one or two won't hurt.' By the end of the journey Alex had chain-smoked his way home and his clothes and the seat were covered in cigarette ash (it took me most of the following morning to vacuum it all away).

Alex mysteriously produced bottles of cider from just about every pocket he had. He was like a magician, pulling one bottle after another from what seemed to be secret recesses of his suit. When and where he had got the cider I haven't a clue, but occasionally through-out the journey home he would offer me a drink. I was a little thirsty and a couple of times I enjoyed a swig of the stuff. Phil was driving, and he declined a drink when Alex thrust a bottle under his nose. Alex was curled up in his seat, seemingly without a care in the world and resting his feet on the dashboard. He was wearing a pair of baseball boots, and on the toe cap of one his son Jordan had sketched a Smiley face.

Alex was living in a terraced cottage at the top of a narrow lane which seemed to disappear into the clouds. As we left him, he gave us his usual farewell: 'Thanks, babes.'

STEPHEN HENDRY

The first time I saw Stephen play was in television's Junior Pot Black, an event I won in 1982 and 1983. Although 14 years of age he was only knee high to a grasshopper, but even then looked a very useful player indeed. He was beaten in the semi-finals by Steve Ventham of Mitcham.

Stephen turned professional in 1986, three years after I had done. Since then he has achieved a great deal, and the world rankings tell the story. As of mid-1991 he is world No.1, and a long way ahead of the rest of us at the top of the charts.

His recent record in ranking tournaments is astonishing: Stephen has proved himself to be a great competitor on the big occasion. I thought Stephen became a world-class player when he defeated Steve Davis in the 1989 UK final. That was the first time he had beaten Steve in a major final and, of course, in a two-day match. It seemed perfectly natural for Stephen to follow that up by winning the World Championship. He was starting to look the complete player, and he went to Sheffield knowing he was in great form. He was a genuine favourite and played like one.

STEVE DAVIS

At his best Steve is the hardest player of all to beat. Stephen Hendry – and Jimmy White, for that matter – can pot you off the table at times; but Steve has a way of screwing you into the ground and keeping you there.

The first time I beat Steve was in the 1989 British Open. It was the seventh time I had played him and after six successive defeats – some of them heavy – I won that match 5–1 to reach the semi-finals. I have a video of the match, and there is no doubt my safety play was a big factor. I had him on the baulk cushion so many times he kept making mistakes and for once I was able to capitalize on them.

He was the absolute business in those days when I kept losing to him. Sometimes he was impossible to play: no matter where you put the cue ball, he either scored points or left you in a worse position. I never seemed able to punish his rare errors. I had the opportunities but didn't take them – and that's fatal against a player of his calibre.

As I grew up with my heart set on becoming a snooker star, Dad would take me as often as possible to watch Steve play if he was in the area. Sometimes that meant a trip along the East Lancs road to Manchester and Potters snooker club. Ever since I first saw Steve play he has always looked the part to me, and at the age of 19 he was in a different class to any of his contemporaries.

If there is a weakness in Steve's game it has taken us a long time to find it. While 1990–91 was not a vintage season for him, I think a lot of that was to do with the fact he had only just got married. It makes a big change to one's life – I know, because it happened to me the previous year. Marriage, a house, and settling down brought about a totally different routine for him.

It's made a big change to Steve's life; and with standards continuing to improve at a time when his own results were not as good as they had been, snooker suddenly became that much more difficult for him.

Meanwhile, Steve already has a tremendous record. His achievement of winning 52 major titles by the end of the 1990–91 season speaks for itself. He is sure to add to that total in the years to come.

Right on Cue

JIMMY WHITE

Jimmy is probably the most natural sportsman I have
ever seen. He is a brilliant player and the fans love
him. I first saw him playing at Pontin's, where he used
to create a stampede when it was known what table he
was playing on. Quite a crowd would gather and wait
patiently for the announcement, 'Jimmy White ...
[pause] ... table six.' Woe betide anyone who stood in
the way of the fans as they charged down the staircase
to the ballroom area where table six was situated.

There is no method to Jimmy's game; no one has ever
coached him. Everything he does is self-taught, which
makes him as natural as anyone you'll ever see. He
might not have been the best safety player in the world
at the outset of his professional career, but he has
developed this part of his game over the years and a
vast improvement has helped him get to where he is
today on the world ranking list. Jimmy is a master at
just clipping balls very thin and when 'on' his safety
game he is very difficult to beat.

Everyone knows how fast he is. While some players
take 10 minutes to put together a 40 break, Jimmy has
won a frame in far less time and probably fired in a
century as well: you can lose frames very quickly
against him.

The 1991 World Championship final is obviously the
match against Jimmy that stands out as far as I'm
concerned. I can't play any better than I did in the first
session, and that demoralized him. I also had a great
match against him in Belgium earlier in the season. I
won that one as well, and it was a pity this was never

shown on television because both of us played so
well.

GARY WILKINSON

I've played Gary four times since he turned professional in 1987 and the score at the moment is two
wins apiece. The last time we met was in the 1990 Dubai
Duty Free Classic, and after I had led 3–0 Gary took
five frames on the trot for a place in the last 16.

Gary has obviously improved a great deal to get as
high as he is on the world ranking list this season, and
he has a solid all-round game. Over the past couple
of years he has also turned in a number of steady
performances.

I can envisage him remaining a fairly high-ranked
player because of the way he plays the game. I didn't
know much about Gary before he turned professional,
though I'd read quite a lot about him in the snooker
magazines.

Gary was probably disappointed with his performance in the 1991 World Championship, when he
lost 13–3 to Jimmy White. He slipped further behind
than he would have liked during the first session and
as the match came to an end I imagine he was still
thinking about the two chances he had missed of
recording a maximum break. It had appeared plain
sailing the first time, but having potted 15 reds and
15 blacks, Gary failed on the yellow. On the second
occasion he missed the last red, so another chance had
gone for the £100,000 jackpot.

143

NEAL FOULDS

Neal and I have been very good friends and rivals since our early teens. He is another player with a very good, solid game, though there are times when his cue action suggests he is not entitled to pot some of the balls he goes for. I'm thinking about those times when he goes for a long shot and his cueing arm goes round his chest. Obviously it works for him, though.

Neal is a good thinker of the game, and he is always difficult to beat. He can also have little spells where he can turn it on and rattle off century after century. I enjoy playing doubles with him because he is a very easy player to get on with. We didn't do too badly to reach the men's doubles semi-finals at the World Masters – even though we then got slaughtered by the Canadians Brady Gollan and Jim Wych.

Neal's game went off somewhat a few years ago owing to domestic problems, and this cost him his place in the top 16. He is back now – and in the top six at that. It only goes to show that you cannot afford to have any distractions in snooker.

STEVE JAMES

Jamesy is a smashing lad who is good company. He is also a tremendous potter. I knew very little about Steve when he turned professional in 1986. The press used to describe him as an ex-postman, but as he got to grips with the professional game it soon became obvious that he was going to be a big threat to all concerned.

144

One of the best matches I have ever been involved in was when I defeated Steve 10–9 in the 1989 Embassy World Championship. I enjoy playing him and I know he enjoys playing me so I suppose our contests will always have a certain amount of zip about them. It won't be for a lack of attacking play that one of us will lose.

Sometimes Steve can knock you a bit sick with some of the balls he pots, but that's the type of player he is. He is certainly a streaky player because once he hits his best form, he is difficult to stop.

Steve's career has blossomed since he teamed up again with Ramsey McLellan (with whom I often have friendly wagers whenever either of the two Liverpool soccer clubs are in action against Manchester City or United. We've also been known to pick a pair of golfers in one of the major events and bet with each other on which one will get the better result.)

Ramsey has a calming influence on Steve and obviously his style of management suits him down to the ground. I'm not sure that Steve's dad, Gordon, has the same effect. Father and son share a passion for powerful motorcycles. At the Crucible this year, Gordon unknowingly left the engine of Steve's BMW car running for a few hours and it burst into flames.

MIKE HALLETT

Mike is a very talented player, and he's another one who pots for fun. There is no great method to his game: he just goes out and plays the way he knows best. He has a good record against me, having won five of our eight matches, so I need to put together a few more wins against him. I get on well with Mike. He and Jan (then his girlfriend) came to my wedding, and Karen and I went to theirs earlier this year.

In many respects Mike is a player rather like Jamesy, and once he gets a streak going he too is difficult to stop. He is a very good one-ball potter – that is, taking on and knocking in the only red that is sticking out. When I was at CueMasters we nicknamed Mike the Kamikaze Kid because of the number of shots he used to take on when the percentages were against him. He took a lot of winding up over this, but you can't deny his results are pretty good.

DENNIS TAYLOR

I always like playing Dennis these days because I always fancy beating him, but that certainly wasn't the case at the outset of my professional career. He used to pulverize me and won four matches in a row before I was able to break my duck.

Dennis in fact was the first player to beat me in the Embassy World Championship when I lost to him 13–11 in 1984. A year later we met in the BCE Canadian Masters and this time I was beaten 5–1 in the first round.

That was the best snooker I had come up against at the time. Dennis went on to win the event by beating Steve Davis 9–4 in the final, and again he played quite magnificently. It's a pity that match has never been

146

shown on television in this country. Dennis made four centuries, three of them in four successive frames, and Steve also threw one in for good measure. In my Canadian Masters match with Dennis I made a 90-odd break in the one frame that I won. In fact, I hardly played a bad shot, but he was too good.

What I had to do now was to develop a game to beat Dennis and it wasn't until the Mercantile Credit Classic in 1988, when I won 5–1 in the quarter-finals, that I played well enough to gain my first victory over him.

Dennis had me – and millions of others – glued to the television set when he won his World Championship on the black in 1985. He really was having a good spell during this period and proved what a tenacious competitor he can be.

He is not the sort of player to give in easily and you only have to look at the 1987 Benson & Hedges final against Alex Higgins for proof of that, Dennis recovering from being 8–5 down to win 9–8. That was a great performance.

DOUG MOUNTJOY

I've played Doug only four times over the years and the last occasion was when he beat me 5–3 in the 1990 Matchroom League. He also defeated me in our third engagement, which came in the semi-finals of the 1989 Dubai Duty Free Classic. I lost 5–4 and wasn't too marvellous at all in that match.

For someone of Doug's age (46), it was a phenomenal

performance to win, and win so well, the two back-to-back ranking events during the 1988–89 season: no one could get close to him. He was superb, particularly against Stephen Hendry in the UK final, in which he made three consecutive centuries. A month later and Doug had also won the Mercantile Credit Classic.

There is no doubt that Frank Callan helped his game at a time when Doug's confidence had sunk very low. Frank made him aware of what he was and what he wasn't doing, and all of a sudden he started to play a bit again and his confidence returned.

TERRY GRIFFITHS

Here is a very, very hard competitor who has to be given every respect on the table. I played Terry four times last season and won only once, though that was the one that mattered as it came in the quarter-finals of the Embassy World Championship. Whatever the occasion we always seem to have good matches.

Terry has a very good safety game to go with his attacking strengths and you know you have been in a match when you've played him. I watched him a lot before I turned professional and even then I could see just how tough an opponent he can be. Since playing him myself I haven't had any reason to change that opinion.

When I beat Terry at Sheffield in April, he told me to keep my game going because I was in the sort of form which could mean it was going to be my year. He said to make sure I controlled the chair and not to let things get to me, which I thought was very nice of him to say. As it turned out, my match with Terry was the hardest one of them all. He kept hanging in and nicking frames: give Terry half a chance and you could live to regret it.

Off the table Terry likes to take the mickey, which has led to plenty of friendly verbal banter between us after some of our matches. The way the Welsh rugby team are playing these days, it's not going to be all that difficult getting one back on our man from Llanelli.

ALAIN ROBIDOUX

I've yet to play Alain at any level, but the fact he is in the top 16 on the world ranking list shows how good a player he is. On the other hand I've witnessed Alain's finger-spinning exploits with the cue ball and these are quite mind boggling. This was one of the better things to come out of the European Open in Deauville. I had so much time off between matches that I was able to watch Alain perform these amazing feats.

It's easy enough to spin the cue through the fingers, I would imagine anyone can do that, but Alain has one or two party pieces up his sleeve. First of all he puts 14 of the 15 reds in their position behind the pink spot, filling the gap left by the odd one out with the black which is slotted into a central position in the triangle.

Alain, standing behind the top cushion and well to the left of the black spot, sends the cue ball spinning out of his hand towards the lower side cushion on the green side of the table and on to the bottom cushion.

The cue ball then spins across to the other lower cushion on the yellow side of the table before it heads straight for the pack of reds and splits them open on making contact.

Easy? Well the plan is to pot the black off three cushions into either top pocket in 30 attempts. I'll tell you something – Alain seldom fails. He has been known to require considerably less than 30 attempts to win his bet, and there are always a few people willing to back against him doing it. I couldn't believe it when I saw him do this for the first time.

Alain also invites bets for another finger-spinning feat in which he does exactly the same again but this time just the pink ball, placed on its spot, is on the table. Usually he will have only 20 attempts to pot it into a top pocket to win the bet.

TONY JONES

Tony Jones, like Gary Wilkinson, is a newcomer to the top 16. When we were amateurs I thought he was just ahead of Neal Foulds and myself. We all turned professional in 1983, but it has taken Tony the longest to climb into the higher positions on the world ranking list.

He has certainly made up for lost time in the last couple of seasons and in 1991 was the surprise winner of the European Open, the event I'd won the two previous years. That was a great performance by Tony, who made sure of a place in the top 16 when he defeated Mike Hallett 10–4 in the first round of the World Championship. Tony has moved from 35th to 15th on the world ranking list and I'm just wondering how many other players have been able to by-pass positions 16–32 in recent years.

EDDIE CHARLTON

I couldn't let an opportunity like this go by without devoting a few words to the veteran Australian, who I owe one for beating me 5–1 in the third round of the 1991 Mercantile Credit Classic.

Eddie celebrates his 62nd birthday on the last day of October and it speaks volumes for his consistency that he has never been out of the top 32 on the world ranking list during a professional career which began over 30 years ago.

Usually when Eddie catches up with me on the circuit he comes out with a little ditty which goes like this: 'Hello, Johnny Parrott, drinks and smokes and messes around with other blokes.' And every time I ask him how he is, Eddie can be relied on to reply: 'If I got any better I couldn't stand it.'

Eddie is a credit to the game. He has always been a difficult player to beat and to have the same old enthusiasm and desire for snooker at his age and to continually play to such a high standard is remarkable.

Most of the players love to watch Eddie at the match table. He is a real character who wouldn't be Steady Eddie if for some reason he chose to stop muttering and swearing under his breath during moments of despair. He does it in such a way you couldn't possibly

151

get the needle with him or take offence. Watch Eddie if his opponent has a big fluke. His face will say a thousand words.

Remember the Hofmeister World Doubles Championship at Northampton in 1987 when Eddie partnered David Taylor? They lost in the fourth round to Dennis Taylor and Cliff Thorburn, but it was during this televised match that Eddie, following a 'lucky' snooker by Dennis, was heard to mutter, 'You jammy pommie....' Of course, neither of Eddie's opponents were pommies, and Dennis and the other players almost doubled up laughing because the only pommie present was Eddie's partner.

JAMES WATTANA

James has done exceptionally well since he turned professional in 1989. He has climbed the ranking list to reach No.20 this season and his achievements are to be commended, bearing in mind he has just turned 21 and has to spend so much time away from his own country. He's certainly lucky to have someone like Tom Moran to look after him. Tom is dedicated to James, has lived in his home country, Thailand, for the past 20 years, and speaks the Thai language fluently. He has helped James to settle down to the British way of life during his visits over here and has also provided sound advice as James improves his knowledge of the English language.

James has already picked up a nickname by continually asking Tom how much money he has earned (he's saving up to buy his mother a house in Thailand). He poses the question at every available opportunity, so we've started calling him 'the Banker'. Judging by his performances at the table, he could well become a 'banker' to win one of the major tournaments in the not too distant future.

STARS OF THE FUTURE

Jonathan Birch, Ken Doherty and Alan McManus are the three young players who most of us expect to reach the top in the years to come. They have just completed their first season in the professional ranks and the future looks decidedly rosy for them.

Alan is just in front on merit (he went down to Terry Griffiths by only 13–12 at Sheffield), but Ken and Jonathan are right behind, and who's to say what this threesome will achieve during the next 12 months?

Take Jonathan. He wasn't helped by illness during his first season but he was still good enough to climb to No.55 on the world ranking list. He also came up against some brilliant performances from his opponents. Neal Foulds, for instance, cleared up with a 62 break to win the ninth and deciding frame on the black in the third round of the Asian Open. Neal had won the eighth frame on the black as well. Jonathan is a player who will definitely improve in the months to come and along with McManus and Doherty can be expected to make further advances towards the top 32 on the world ranking list during 1991–92.

I saw Ken Doherty play last year for the first time,

and he impressed me enormously. I think he's going to be an exceptionally good player. His performance in the World Championships this year, where he was 8–6 ahead of Steve Davis before losing 10–8 was remarkable. He was 4–0 behind at one point before going on to lead 8–6, and there's not many people who can do that to Steve.

REFEREES

I have always had an excellent relationship with the referees. John Williams, Alan Chamberlain, Len Ganley, John Street, Vic Bartlam and – more frequently in previous years – John Smyth are the officials I'm referring to; and let's not forget our markers and scorers, such as Jim Furlong, Jim Coupland and Paul Fisher, and press officer Colin Randle, whose past duties used to involve operating the switches which control the electronic scoreboards.

There is a special relationship between John Williams and myself, mainly because of our association with Pontin's. 'John Willie', as he is affectionately known, is the man responsible for the smooth running of the tournaments at the holiday camps and the fact there are rarely any hitches is due to his efficient organization. His wife Kathy is often with John at Pontin's and at major events, and Phil and myself have got to know them quite well.

In recent seasons I have also had a great rapport with Len Ganley, who has been with me on a number of overseas trips. We take the mickey out of each other

154

relentlessly, and Len has a huge following among the snooker public.

Len though is a bit of a wheeler-dealer, and if you need something, the chances are that he will be able to get it for you or put you in touch with someone who can.

A familiar figure at all the major events is our compere Alan Hughes who has a very professional approach to his duties. Alan, like myself, is keen on horse racing and we often discuss 'form' backstage or during relaxing moments. Alan likes a flutter and it's a picture to see him when he's on a winner. Many fans of the 'noble art' will have seen Alan at Barry Hearn's boxing promotions. He does all the introductions and announces the judges' scores at the big fights in the inimitable style which has made him so popular in the snooker arena.

A word about our tournament director, Ann Yates, who until a couple of years ago was the WPBSA's press officer. I've grown up with Ann, so to speak, as she started out on the circuit just before I became a professional. I've got to know her well over the years and she has always been pleasant and helpful to me. Ann has a very demanding job in the male-dominated world of snooker, and no one could deny she is making a success of it.

18

Pot Black

In August 1991 the return of Junior Pot Black to the television screen brought back pleasant memories of my two victories in this event, when it was staged at the Pebble Mill Studios in Birmingham. I won in 1982 and again a year later. The final was decided by the aggregate score of only two frames – but that couldn't detract from one's great sense of achievement at being a winner.

The tournament was first held in 1981, but after the 1983 final it was taken off the screens until 1991. The format in 1981 was different to that in later years. Twelve players took part in this first event and after a sudden death knock-out involving all of us, the six winners were divided into two groups of three. A round robin followed, the top two players in each group going through to the semi-finals. Dean Reynolds and Dene O'Kane qualified from one group, and Gregg Jenkins of Australia and I from the other group. The final involved Dean Reynolds and Dene O'Kane, two of today's leading professionals. Dean became the first Junior Pot Black champion with an aggregate score of 151 to 79.

To win Junior Pot Black in 1982 I defeated John Keers of Newcastle in the final, while a year later I retained the trophy by beating Steve Ventham of Mitcham. In each of the three years I participated I compiled the highest break: 98 in 1981, 56 in 1982 and 71 in 1983.

I can't resist quoting what Ted Lowe had to say about Junior Pot Black in the October 1982 issue of *Cue World* (a snooker magazine which ceased publication in 1989), when he reviewed the series which had taken place that year. He wrote: 'Are we to see future champions out of this year's tournament? In my view one name which stands out is eighteen-year-old John Parrott, a six foot one and a half inches tall Liverpudlian who seems to have every attribute to become world champion. He's already notched up the North West junior title, reached the final of this year's Northern championship and was a finalist in the British Under-19's. It was no mean feat when young Parrott beat Ray Reardon in the final of the 1982 Pontin's Open.'

Thanks for the testimonial, Ted – and I'm delighted to have proved you right!

The players who took part in the Junior Pot Black series during the 1980s were as follows: 1981 – Dean Reynolds, Dene O'Kane, Neal Foulds, John Keers, Jon White, Danny Adds, Mark Bennett, Tony Pyle, Terry Whitthread, Paul Ennis, Greg Jenkins, and me. 1982 – Neal Foulds, Paddy Browne, Jon White, John Keers, Steve Ventham, Mark Lockwood, Chris Hamson and me. 1983 – Steve Ventham, John Keers, Chris Hamson, Stephen Hendry, Mark Thompson, Brian Rowswell,

Nick Pearce and me. (I wasn't due to play in the tournament in 1983 but was called in at the 11th hour when Paddy Browne dropped out after breaking a foot playing football.) Two referees have taken charge of Junior Pot Black: John Williams (1981–82) and Vic Bartlam. It was Vic who also refereed my Pontin's Junior final in 1981.

From the competitors' point of view, Junior Pot Black was very exciting, particularly the prospect of playing in front of the television cameras for the first time. I must confess I was very nervous at the outset, but the experience stood me (and my fellow future professionals) in good stead when we were later involved in the televised rounds of the major tournaments. I often have a laugh with Stephen Hendry about his appearance in the 1983 event. He was a wee lad in those days, and when it was his turn to come to the table, he had to slide off his chair because his feet didn't reach the floor!

Some of the old footage from Junior Pot Black was shown on television this summer. Stephen, who was twelve at the time, was asked by the interviewer what he felt when his opponent potted the final black to win the frame. Stephen has confided to me, 'I felt like crying and saying "I want me mum!"' Nerve-wracking it might have been, but it's good to see this series has been brought back, along with Pot Black. There will always be a place for Pot Black on television, which returned in September 1991 after a five-year absence. The series kept the game going in the years when it was very much a minority sport. Today snooker gives an enormous amount of pleasure to millions of people.

Pot Black

Pot Black is a difficult tournament to win because in a one-frame match you do need to have a good run of the balls. The series was first televised in 1969, when snooker was very much in the doldrums. Ted Lowe, the BBC commentator in every series of Pot Black and Junior Pot Black, makes no secret of the fact that in those days there were so few professionals around it wasn't easy to find eight who could play in the event.

Pot Black played a major part in helping to put snooker back on the map. The series was given an enormous boost with the coming of colour television. The first Pot Black recordings were made at the BBC's Gosta Green studios in Birmingham. The most recent ones took place at Trentham Gardens, Stoke-on-Trent, where so much top-rank snooker was played during the summer of 1991.

I played in the last two Pot Black series in 1985 and 1986 but failed to win a match. Jimmy White, who won the 1986 Pot Black, defeated me in 1985 and Dennis Taylor sent me packing 12 months later. In 1991 I managed to beat Tony Knowles in the first round but then lost to Doug Mountjoy for a place in the semi-finals.

Eddie Charlton holds the Pot Black highest break record. He made a 110 during the 1973 tournament. I recall Eddie presenting me with the snooker balls with which I made the 98 break in my very first Junior Pot Black.

Only three referees have officiated at Pot Black. Bruce Donkin, who used to be the Master of Ceremonies at the Embassy World Championship, was in charge in the inaugural series in 1969. The late Sydney

Lee was the referee from 1970 to 1979 inclusive, while John Williams has refereed every series from 1980 onwards.

19

Snooker Calendar

The 1991–92 snooker season, for the top eight players on the world ranking list plus Dennis Taylor, Terry Griffiths and James Wattana, began in earnest in the Far East in August with events in Thailand, Hong Kong and India. We were away for nearly three weeks, and then within four days of returning to England most of us had packed our bags again and headed for Scotland to take part in the Regal Scottish Masters, which is held in the concert hall at Motherwell Civic Centre.

This is a very tough tournament to win. It was first held in 1989 at the Scottish Exhibition Centre in Glasgow and moved to its new home in Motherwell a year later. Stephen Hendry won both those events in front of his home crowd, so obviously it suits him down to the ground. I always go by road to Scotland rather than take the shuttle from Manchester airport. I quite like the drive north and certainly prefer to go in that direction rather than the other on the M6.

The Scottish tournament was followed by the fourth and fifth rounds of the Dubai Duty Free Classic at Trentham Gardens, Stoke-on-Trent, the scene of so much snooker activity during the summer months. It

161

must have been quite a hectic time for the referees and officials as the first three rounds of nine of the 10 world ranking events scheduled for the 1991–92 season were also played at this venue.

The fields for the Dubai Duty Free Classic and, later, the Asian and European Opens, the Regal Welsh Open and the Strachan Professional each had to be reduced to the last 16 before the eight tables being used at Trentham Gardens could finally be taken down at the beginning of October.

There was, however, a long enough break in September between the fourth and fifth rounds of the Dubai Duty Free Classic and the fourth and fifth rounds of the Asian Open for me to play in the Belgian Masters at Antwerp, one of Barry Hearn's five World Series tournaments. The venue, the Sporthal Schijnpoort, is next door to the Schijnpoort Snooker Centre, where we all eat and practise. The owner, Frank van Dyck, and his wife Machteld have already become good friends of all of us. The Belgian event is well organized and, since I've won there, you could say the venue is right up my street.

From Antwerp it's back to qualifying at Trentham Gardens. The last thing you want now is to fall ill or suffer an injury. The four events which still have to be reduced to the last 16 take place back-to-back, which means that a punishing schedule faces us all. In view of the number of players there are in the professional ranks today and the number of matches that have to be arranged, I don't suppose there is any better way of playing these rounds. But it's vitally important to be in peak condition: a bad week at Trentham Gardens could mean trouble for the rest of the season.

The first ranking event to be played to a finish is the Dubai Duty Free Classic. Those of us who have been to Dubai know what a lovely place this is; it's definitely one of my favourite overseas trips. This season the prize for a 147 maximum break is a luxury Mercedes 500SL or a BMW 825i costing around £86,000 – so if any of us finds himself needing just the final black to collect, he'll be twitching just a fraction when he lines up the shot.

At Dubai we play in the Al Nasr Stadium, an excellent indoor sports arena. It's very warm in the Middle East at this time of the year, but the air conditioning is excellent and at our hotel a dip in the swimming pool gives you the chance to cool down. We are always well looked after by the sponsors, Dubai Duty Free, and the snooker venue is right next to the football stadium, where Liverpool and Celtic have played. There were great celebrations during the first year the Dubai Duty Free Classic was held in 1989 because the United Arab Emirates football team (Dubai is one of the Emirates) qualified for the 1990 World Cup finals in Italy – a remarkable performance. The mind boggles at the rewards the players received after a draw in their final match against North Korea enabled them to make the trip to Italy (the zonal favourites China were beaten by Qatar on the same day). According to reliable reports, each player was given a house, a car, a Rolex watch and £10,000 as a bonus!

After Dubai, it's back home and then to Reading for the Rothmans Grand Prix, which is always held at the Hexagon, a tremendous venue. I haven't done very well in this event. My best performance was in 1987, when I reached the semi-finals. But it's a pleasure to play at the Hexagon and the Rothmans is a very prestigious event to win. It's also very convenient for me because my mother lives not far from Oxford. I usually stay with her during this tournament: it's home from home.

One year the players all stayed at the nearby Ramada Hotel – and on three consecutive nights we had a bomb scare. It was ridiculous. I remember Dennis Taylor telling me he was engrossed in a film on TV about poltergeists, and when the alarm went off he thought for a minute it had something to do with what he was watching.

Eventually Dennis, like the rest of us, headed for safety, taking care to pick up his wallet and cue as he left his room. On two occasions we were herded into the social club at the local police station, where we stayed for over an hour before being allowed to return to the hotel. It must have been extraordinary to see so many people – some wearing their nightclothes underneath coats, mackintoshes, even blankets – walking the streets of Reading at 4am. One consolation for the drinkers was that the management at the Ramada provided a complimentary top-up on their return.

After the Rothmans, there are a few days off in which to re-charge one's batteries before the UK Championship at Preston Guild Hall. This is a terrific venue for me because it's really just down the road from my house. The Guild Hall is also a great place to play: there's plenty of atmosphere and the event is second in importance only to the Embassy World Championship.

The matches at Preston, for the first time in the

season, are over 17 frames, and these longer games suit me much better. There is much less need to worry if you lose the first two or three frames, though obviously you don't want that to happen. I've never made it through to the UK final, which has disappointed me a bit; but I've been in the semis a couple of times, on the last occasion in 1990 when I lost to Steve Davis.

The UK Championship is followed by two more events before Christmas – the World Matchplay at Brentwood and the last leg of Barry Hearn's World Series in Monte Carlo.

I've been in two World Matchplay finals and lost both, one to Davis and the other to Jimmy White. The venue at Brentwood is a leisure centre which is specially prepared for the snooker. I like it: the atmosphere is good and again the matches are over the 17-frame distance, apart from the final, which is now played over 35 frames.

We had a problem getting to Brentwood in 1990 owing to the snow. Parts of the Midlands section of the M6 was blocked, so Phil and I detoured via the M5 before picking up the M4 at Bristol and heading for the M25 and Essex. Quite a journey, that was.

I enjoy Monte Carlo quite apart from having to play snooker there, so it should be good fun to round off the World Series 555 Challenge in the principality. In its visits to Monte Carlo, the Parrott party invariably enjoys the kindness, hospitality and excellent organization of Snooker International's Dennis Thompson-Panther, Danielle de Capele and their capable personal assistant, Inger Haugland, who are all based there. We are in Monte Carlo until 22 December, so it's important to do the Christmas shopping before the event.

New Year's Day sees the start of the Mercantile Credit Classic at the Bournemouth International Centre. From a travel point of view this is the worst venue of all for me. I haven't done very well there, either, losing to Eddie Charlton in 1990 and hardly excelling when England lost to the Republic of Ireland in the 1990 World Team Cup. But this in no way detracts from the centre itself. It's a nice venue and Bournemouth is a nice place to visit – even though my stays there have usually been a little too short.

The Mercantile Credit is followed by the Asian Open in Bangkok. In the past it's been held earlier in the season, but this time we go there in January. Thankfully the venue is at the hotel where we are staying. Bangkok traffic is hell, and to travel even a couple of miles can take over three hours – as Terry Griffiths discovered during the 1991 Thai Masters. At least the locals are friendly and helpful.

A new ranking event, the Regal Welsh Masters, is scheduled for February, but before that the prestigious Benson & Hedges Masters takes place at Wembley Conference Centre. The first time I played at Wembley I was amazed at the layout of the arena. Compared with other venues, the table seemed so far from where the players sat, I was waiting for a bus to come by and give me a lift. When Wembley is full, the atmosphere is superb – though the spectators at the back are so far away I'm sure they need binoculars to view the action. But it is a great set-up and a great event run so competently over the years first by Len Owen and these

166

days by Jim Elkin, who is ably assisted by Suzy Lewis and Sheila Mercer.

The Conference Centre is always spotless, all the players love to be involved in the tournament, and the actual venue is rather like an enlarged soup bowl version of the Crucible Theatre. I remember beating Jimmy White there on the pink one Friday night. There was a huge crowd of over 2,000, and of course the vast majority were rooting for him. I've also been in two finals at Wembley so, although Stephen Hendry beat me both times, I have to say I like playing there.

There is another Benson & Hedges-sponsored tournament. This is the Irish Masters, which is the last major before the Embassy World Championship. The Irish B&H is held at Goffs, Co. Kildare, and to my mind this venue is only a short head in quality behind the Crucible Theatre. It's one event you always want to go back to. The hospitality extended by the Irish is second to none, and Kevin Norton, who organizes the tournament, does everything impeccably. He has a huge team of helpers, everything runs like clockwork and nothing is too much trouble for any of them.

As for Goffs itself, it has an atmosphere all its own: it's the only place I know of where you actually pay to stand. The Irish love their snooker, and it's a pity a world ranking event isn't held in this part of the world. Goffs, incidentally, is where some of the world's best thoroughbred racehorses are sold. When you attend a sale there, it's difficult to imagine that same ring being used as a snooker arena.

I must confess that on the occasion when I went to the sales with Ray Edmonds I thought for one heart-stopping moment I had purchased a yearling colt by Northern Dancer for something adjacent to £1.3 million. As the auctioneer conducted the bidding I scratched my nose. He happened to be looking in my direction at the time and, pointing towards me, said, '£1.3 over there.' I was in a state of panic until I happened to glance round and saw that the well-known owner Robert Sangster was standing behind me and that it was he whose bid the auctioneer had acknowledged.

I'm one of only a few players who have played at Goffs and attended the sales there. I've also been to the races at the nearby Naas track, which is known as the punter's graveyard – an apt description, believe me! People who talk about Sunday racing should go to Naas. The place was heaving; it was packed.

Sandwiched between the two Benson & Hedges tournaments are the Regal Welsh Open, the Pearl Assurance British Open, the European Open and the Strachan Professional, which are all completed within a five-week period during February and March.

The Welsh event, the first world ranking tournament to be played in Wales, is held at the Newport Leisure Centre. This is where the Welsh Professional Championship used to be played, so for players like Terry Griffiths and Doug Mountjoy it's familiar territory. I have played very little snooker in Wales, so if I'm lucky enough to reach the last 16 of the Regal, it will make quite a refreshing change.

The Pearl Assurance British Open returns to its usual venue at the Derby Assembly Rooms, where the spectators watch either from tiered seating at ground-floor level or from the balcony. My record at Derby is pretty mixed. I've been in two semi-finals, but I've also made some early exits from the event. The Assembly Rooms is a good venue, though, and I enjoy playing there.

I'm seeded No. 1 for the Strachan Professional. This is another new ranking event and, like the Regal Welsh, has been warmly welcomed by the professionals. And the 1991 European Open looks like being played at a venue I haven't been to – the Imax Theatre in Rotterdam, which has received the thumbs up from everyone who has played there. (My European Open victories, as we've already seen, were at Deauville in 1989 and Lyon in 1990.)

The final event of the season is the Embassy World Championship – the big one – at the Crucible Theatre in Sheffield. This is the best tournament to win and it's played at the best venue in the world. No other arena can boast such an electric atmosphere.

My Dad and I were at the Crucible during the 1979 Embassy World Championship. Mike Watterson, who promoted the tournament at that time, provided us with a couple of tickets to watch Cliff Thorburn's match from the press seats, which in those days were at the side of the main auditorium. Cliff knocked in a break of 125 and in its later stages you could have cut the atmosphere with a knife. 'What a place this is!' I thought – never imagining that five years later I would be playing there myself.

I'm often asked what it's like to walk out from behind the curtain and be introduced to the audience at the Crucible. Well, the first thing is to make sure you don't fall down the steps. As I've mentioned before, they are a bit steep, so you have to watch where your feet are going. But the view from the top of those steps is one of the great sights in the world of professional snooker.

For several years my season concluded with the Pontin's tournament which follows immediately after the World Championship. Sadly today, owing to the pressure of my commitments, I am no longer able to accept the customary invitation to Prestatyn. I did in fact go back for a day in 1991 to show the World Championship trophy to Walter Rowley, John Rutherford and Alan Jones, who over the years have had so much to do with snooker at Pontin's. It was the least I could do to repay all the help they have given me.

20

Burn-out

As you might imagine after reading the previous chapter, it's impossible for any player to maintain his very best form from the beginning of the season right through to the end. I'm involved in 20 or more tournaments during the 1991–92 season, and the idea of playing at my best, week in and week out, is just not on. It's the same, I believe, for all the other top players.

The question of burn-out – a mixture of physical and mental fatigue – certainly has to come into our calculations when planning for the new season. Snooker is becoming more and more international, the seasonal calendar is getting longer and longer, and tournaments are taking place not only in the UK, the Republic of Ireland and mainland Europe but in far-distant countries like Hong Kong, Thailand, China and India.

It can all add up to a demanding schedule. I'm certainly not complaining at the position I'm in, but I believe more and more of us, particularly those in the top eight on the world ranking list, will be looking hard and long at future plans and, perhaps, not entering quite as many events as we have done in the past.

I'm fortunate to be where I am, earning a good living from the game. It's a fact of life that not every player is as good as the next and that some are naturally better than others. But in the supercharged world of professional snooker it could be harmful to have too much of a good thing. The time is approaching when some players won't mind getting knocked out of some tournaments at an early stage.

There are at present 10 ranking events, along with World Series and various invitation tournaments. I like to play whenever possible and don't enjoy turning down invitations – but how far should you go beyond the point where, mentally, you've had enough? A factor in my victory in this year's World Championship was my lousy form in the three months preceding it. I was the freshest horse in the race at Sheffield because of my early departure from many of the events leading up to it.

The Far East World Series tour which launched the 1991–92 season for 11 of the leading players was hectic to say the least. It involved no less than six journeys by air, the first being the shuttle from Manchester to Heathrow. Then came an 11-hour flight to Bangkok, followed by hops to Hong Kong and finally India, before we boarded a British Airways jumbo for the long haul home and the shuttle again to Manchester. It was a very demanding 19 days, but we did get the sort of concentrated match practice that would prove useful as the season got underway.

I got beaten early on in Hong Kong. I wasn't too upset over this as the Crown Colony is one of my favourite places overseas; there's so much to do there, and it's much more westernized than Thailand or India.

However, somewhere on the tour I picked up the dreaded 'Delhi-belly'. In all I lost about 10 pounds in weight, and on one occasion completed *The Times* crossword while camped in the bathroom. I had taken every precaution I could think of to avoid this bug, even going as far as to eat nothing more than dry toast, boiled eggs and tomato soup. When the doctor came to see me he told me I had colitis. He gave me some tablets and told me there was also a strict diet to follow: dried toast, boiled eggs and tomato soup! I knocked the soup and eggs off the menu, and existed on dried toast and bottled water for the next five days.

Of course for us Brits countries like India are so different from the foreign parts we are more accustomed to. We are just not used to the climate and the conditions there. The smell in the hotels was the same everywhere: it was camphor, which is put down to keep away the cockroaches.

As far as the snooker was concerned, the tables in India played very well, and there were a number of century breaks, which the excellent crowds really appreciated. They certainly had plenty to cheer about and it was encouraging to see how keen the Indian public are about snooker.

The Hong Kong event was also well supported, which is more than you can say for Thailand during the early rounds. There wasn't a single spectator for one of my matches on the No. 2 table – everyone had rushed over to the No. 1 table, which was set out for television.

I played Stephen Hendry in the final at the Taj Mahal Hotel in Delhi. Although he beat me 9–5 I was quite pleased with the way my game had developed over the three-week period.

But, to come back to the main point of this chapter, long overseas trips can bring you to your knees. If the calendar is as congested for 1992–93, Phil and I will be taking a close look at the diary and weighing up all the pros and cons of participating in each event.

21

The Press

Over the years I think that I, like most of my fellow professionals, have built up a very good rapport with the snooker press, some of whom spend more time on the circuit than others.

If there is a problem it usually arises when news hounds arrive on the scene to sniff out a tip-off. But they stand out like a sore thumb, and the players are very wary of them. The snooker reporters are a different breed of journalist, and I have got to know many of them well on a personal level. What with all the travelling involved on the circuit these days, it must be just as difficult for them as it is for us. Some members of the snooker press have been on the circuit longer than I've been a professional, and when you spend so much time in each other's company you obviously get to know each other very well.

I don't think I've ever taken serious exception to anything written about me, and the snooker press does a good job promoting the image of the game.

Terry Smith, the editor of *Pot Black* and a former snooker correspondent of the *Daily Telegraph,* is one of the press regulars. He's good company and can be guaranteed to raise a laugh or two. Over the years Terry has built up a reputation for being a bit clumsy in the press room, and now it never surprises his colleagues if he accidentally demolishes the odd table, chair or partition.

On the recent trip to India, Terry took with him bottles of mineral water, tea bags and ginger biscuits so that he could enjoy a typical English brew. He is finicky about his food: anything other than normal English fare is dismissed as 'foreign muck.'

Terry had a shock when he ordered steak and chips, with no trimmings, at our hotel in India. It turned out that the hotel had run out of steak, and served him a portion of water buffalo instead. His response on learning this wouldn't have been out of place in *Fawlty Towers*. (In the end Terry was able to overcome his hunger pangs by popping round to the British High Commission for sausage, egg and baked beans.)

When he checked out of the hotel in India he almost went bananas on learning his phone bill was over £1,000 more than he had calculated. It turned out that an intruder had been using his room while he was out to make a whole series of world-wide phone calls.

A famous tale about Terry concerns the time when, arriving late at an airport, he rushed across the tarmac and climbed one of those portable staircases to board an Aer Lingus flight to Dublin. It was only when he he got to the top of the stairs that he discovered the aircraft was 40 yards away. As he sheepishly descended the staircase Terry was met by a steward, who warned him sternly, 'You have just failed the Aer Lingus initiative test!'

Joe Lancaster, the Manchester freelance, is another member of the snooker press who has been around for a long time. I can always wind him up with a tale about Manchester United – though I've got to be careful because Joe will relay the story to one of his newspapers if I don't let on that I'm only kidding. One of the old school, Joe loves his football and athletics as well as snooker, and it's a racing certainty he'll be in Barcelona for the Olympics in 1992.

Steve Acteson, who now works exclusively for *Today* but until the 1991–92 season was snooker correspondent of both *Today* and *The Times,* is the Mike Yarwood of the press room. Some of his impersonations are uncanny and if you ever have occasion to hear Alex Higgins' voice without actually seeing him, there's a good chance that it's Steve rather than the 'People's Champion' who's doing the talking. His take-off of Alex is so real that many of us have been fooled by an Acteson phone call. One notable victim was Danny Bratt (now one of Barry Hearn's Matchroom men), who at the time was a novice radio reporter at the Crucible and fell hook, line and sinker for the 'Higgins' chat.

Steve also does excellent impersonations of Ray Reardon and David Taylor. He's even tried me, but so far he's failed miserably to master the Liverpool accent. He sounds more like a Brummie. I'll have to give him some lessons.

The *Daily Mirror*'s Tony Stenson is one of those lovable pressmen you couldn't possibly fall out with even if he misquoted you. According to his press room rivals he has a habit of making up the odd quote here and there. Well, I think they are just envious – I don't

believe a word of it! I walked into the press room one
day wearing a shell suit and Tony remarked, 'Haven't
you got an iron in your house?' I fell about laughing
at that one. But the best comment he made was at a
Cliff Thorburn interview at the Embassy World Championship in 1987. Cliff had lost 10–5 to Dene O'Kane in
the first round after leading 5–1. For a moment or two
Cliff sat quietly in front of the press; no-one was keen
to ask him anything about the débâcle. Then Tony
piped up: 'Well, Cliff, is this the first time you've lost
nine frames on the trot?' Cliff answered dryly, 'No, it's
about the 10th or 11th.'

On another occasion Tony, always looking for a sen-
sational story, asked Barry Hearn: 'Can we call Neal
Fould's heart murmur a heart attack?' Barry gave him
a fairly succinct reply.

The *Sun*'s Alisdair Ross can be quite a comedian
when he wants to. When he acted as Framework's press
officer on the tour to China, Ally invented a whole raft
of typical *Sun*-style headlines like 'Snooker Star Found
in Chinese Love Nest', and 'Parrott's Peking Pranks'.
Ally can get carried away a little when he's had a glass
or two, but basically he's great company.

Clive Everton, the doyen of snooker journalists, is
editor of *Snooker Scene*. He is also, of course, a BBC
television commentator, writes for the *Sunday Times*
and *Guardian,* and is a professional player who serves
on the board of the WPBSA.

Clive has his enemies. He and his assistant editor,
Janice Hale, undoubtedly get involved in contentious
issues but usually some good sense emerges from their
arguments in the end. Snooker needs someone like

Clive who, after all, has been involved with our sport for many, many years. You have to respect his views even if you don't always agree with them.

The Press Association's correspondent is Bruce Beckett, who usually turns up at every venue with one valuable piece of equipment: not a notebook and pencil but a snooker cue. No one in the press corps is keener to play a game of snooker or pool, and whenever his demanding PA duties allow, he will pop off to the local snooker club for a game or two. Bruce has won a few press room tournaments, but I don't think he has any intention of trying his luck on the professional circuit.

Finally, there is John Dee, the voice of CueCall, snooker's only regular 0898 telephone number. We have known each other ever since I competed as a junior at Pontin's and he has helped me to piece together this autobiography. I am greatly appreciative of his untiring efforts. I recall that when John was writing his preview of the 1990 Embassy World Championship for the *Wolverhampton Express & Star,* I was his selection for the winner. Well, he was only one year out!

22

Head to Head

John Parrott made his professional début in the 1983 Professional Players Tournament at the Masters Club, near Stockport. He defeated his first opponent, Paul Watchorn of Dublin, 5–0 and the tournament then moved to Redwood Lodge, Bristol, where he had a 5–2 win over Patsy Fagan before losing 5–1 to Terry Griffiths for a place in the last 16.

His playing record against the top 32 on the world ranking list for the 1991–92 season and a few other players, along with his main achievements throughout his playing career so far, are as follows:

John Parrott v Stephen Hendry (World ranking 1)
Parrott wins (7)

6–3 SF 1988 Pontin's Professional
9–6 SF 1988 World Matchplay
9–8 SF 1989 World Matchplay
10–6 F 1990 European Open
5–3 SF 1990 Humo Belgian Masters
4–2 SF 1990 Norwich Union Grand Prix
5–3 1990 Matchroom League

Hendry wins (9)

5–3 Rd 3 1986 International
9–7 SF 1987 Rothmans Grand Prix
9–6 F 1989 Benson & Hedges Masters
5–3 1989 Matchroom League
6–4 SF 1989 Regal Scottish Masters
4–2 F 1989 Continental Airlines London Masters
9–4 F 1990 Benson & Hedges Masters
16–11 SF 1990 Embassy World Championship
4–2 F 1990 Continental Airlines London Masters

John Parrott v Steve Davis (World ranking 2)
Parrott wins (4)

5–1 QF 1989 British Open
6–2 SF 1990 Benson & Hedges Masters
4–2 F 1990 Norwich Union Grand Prix
16–10 SF 1991 Embassy World Championship

Davis wins (10)

5–4 SF 1984 Lada Classic
5–4 QF 1984 Mercantile Credit Classic
9–5 QF 1987 UK Championship
13–11 F 1988 Mercantile Credit Classic
9–4 QF 1988 UK Championship
9–5 F 1988 World Matchplay
5–3 1989 Matchroom League
18–3 F 1989 Embassy World Championship
9–6 SF 1990 UK Championship
4–3 SF 1991 Continental Airlines London Masters
9–5 F 1991 Benson & Hedges Irish Masters

Draws (1)

4–4 1990 Matchroom League.

John Parrott v Jimmy White (World ranking 3)
Parrott wins (6)

5–4 QF 1989 Benson & Hedges Masters
5–1 QF 1989 Benson & Hedges Irish Masters
13–7 QF 1989 Embassy World Championship
9–6 F 1990 Humo Belgian Masters
4–1 Rd 1 1990 Norwich Union Grand Prix
18–11 F 1991 Embassy World Championship

White wins (5)

5–3 SF 1985 Carlsberg Challenge
13–8 Rd 2 1986 Embassy World Championship
13–11 Rd 2 1978 Embassy World Championship
18–9 F 1989 World Matchplay
5–3 1990 Matchroom League

Draws (1)

4–4 1989 Matchroom League.

John Parrott v Gary Wilkinson (World ranking 5)
Parrott wins (2)

5–2 Rd 4 1989 European Open
5–1 Rd 4 1989 Rothmans Grand Prix

Wilkinson wins (2)

9–6 Rd 5 1989 UK Championship
5–3 Rd 4 1990 Dubai Duty Free Classic

John Parrott v Neal Foulds (World ranking 6)
Parrott wins (5)

5–4 Rd 1 1988 Benson & Hedges Masters
5–0 Rd 5 1988 British Open
6–5 SF 1989 Benson & Hedges Masters

5–4 SF 1989 English Championship
5–3 1989 Matchroom League

Foulds wins (2)

9–3 SF 1986 UK Championship
7–1 1990 Matchroom League

John Parrott v Steve James (World ranking 7)
Parrott wins (3)

10–9 Rd 1 1989 Embassy World Championship
5–3 Rd 5 1989 Dubai Duty Free Classic
6–3 SF 1990 European Open

James wins (2)

5–3 Rd 5 1990 Mercantile Credit Classic
5–3 QF 1990 Rothmans Grand Prix

John Parrott v Mike Hallett (World ranking 8)
Parrott wins (4)

9–1 F 1988 Pontin's Professional
5–4 SF 1989 European Open
5–4 Rd 1 1989 Norwich Union Grand Prix
4–1 Rd 1 1990 Continental Airlines London Masters

Hallett wins (5)

6–5 SF 1988 Benson & Hedges Masters
9–8 SF 1988 British Open
5–3 Rd 1 1988 Fosters Professional
5–3 QF 1988 BCE Canadian Masters
9–7 F 1989 English Championship

John Parrott v Dennis Taylor (World ranking 9)
Parrott wins (7)

    5–1 QF 1988 Mercantile Credit Classic
    9–4 Rd 5 1988 UK Championship
    5–1 Rd 1 1989 Benson & Hedges Masters
    5–1 Rd 1 1989 Benson & Hedges Irish Masters
    13–10 Rd 2 1989 Embassy World Championship
    9–6 QF 1989 World Matchplay
    6–2 SF 1991 Benson & Hedges Irish Masters

Taylor wins (5)

    13–11 Rd 2 1984 Embassy World Championship
    5–2 Rd 2 1985 British Open
    5–1 QF 1985 International
    5–1 Rd 1 1985 BCE Canadian Masters
    3–1 Rd 1 1988 LEP Hong Kong Masters

Draws (1)

    4–4 1990 Matchroom League

John Parrott v Doug Mountjoy (World ranking 10)
Parrott wins (2)

    5–4 QRd 1984 Lada Classic
    5–2 Rd 5 1989 British Open

Mountjoy wins (2)

    5–4 SF 1989 Dubai Duty Free Classic
    5–3 1990 Matchroom League

John Parrott v Terry Griffiths (World ranking 11)
Parrott wins (6)

    5–1 Rd 5 1985 International
    5–4 Rd 5 1987 Rothmans Grand Prix
    9–8 F 1989 European Open

5–3 1989 Matchroom League
5–1 Rd 1 1990 Humo Belgian Masters
13–10 QF 1991 Embassy World Championship

Griffiths wins (5)

5–1 Rd 2 1983 Professional Players Tournament
5–3 QF 1990 Benson & Hedges Irish Masters
6–3 QF 1990 Regal Scottish Masters
9–8 QF 1990 World Matchplay
5–2 QF 1991 Benson & Hedges Masters

John Parrott v Dean Reynolds (World ranking 12)
Parrott wins (3)

5–0 QF 1988 Pontin's Professional
4–2 SF 1988 Kent Cup
13–11 Rd 2 1990 Embassy World Championship

Reynolds wins (3)

6–2 Rd 4 1988 English Championship
9–8 SF 1989 British Open
5–2 Rd 5 1989 Rothmans Grand Prix

John Parrott v Alain Robidoux (World ranking 13)
No matches

John Parrott v Martin Clark (World ranking 14)
Parrott wins (1)

5–1 F 1988 Kent Cup (China)

Clark wins (0)

John Parrott v Tony Jones (World ranking 15)
Parrott wins (2)

5–2 Rd 3 1987 Mercantile Credit Classic

9–3 Rd 4 1990 UK Championship

Jones wins (0)

John Parrott v Tony Knowles (World ranking 16)
Parrott wins (8)

    5–1 QF 1984 Lada Classic
    10–7 Rd 1 1984 Embassy World Championship
    9–4 QF 1986 UK Championship
    9–4 Rd 5 1987 UK Championship
    9–4 SF 1988 Mercantile Credit Classic
    5–2 Rd 5 1989 BCE International
    9–7 QF 1990 UK Championship
    13–1 Rd 2 1991 Embassy World Championship

Knowles wins (1)

    6–3 Rd 1 1989 Lion Brown New Zealand Masters

John Parrott v Willie Thorne (World ranking 17)
Parrott wins (3)

    5–0 QF 1985 Winfield Masters
    5–3 1989 Matchroom League
    5–3 Rd 2 1991 Benson & Hedges Masters

Thorne wins (1)

    9–7 Rd 1 1984 UK Championship

Draws (1)

    4–4 1990 Matchroom League

John Parrott v Dene O'Kane (World ranking 18)
Parrott wins (2)

    5–2 QF 1988 British Open

5–2 Rd 5 1990 Rothmans Grand Prix

O'Kane wins (0)

John Parrott v Peter Francisco (World ranking 19)
Parrott wins (2)

5–1 QF 1988 Dubai Duty Free Classic
5–0 Rd 4 1990 Asian Open

Francisco wins (0)

John Parrott v James Wattana (World ranking 20)
Parrott wins (2)

5–3 Rd 4 1989 Dubai Duty Free Classic
4–1 Rd 1 1991 Continental Airlines London Masters

Wattana wins (0)

John Parrott v Nigel Bond (World ranking 21)
Parrott wins (2)

5–3 QF 1990 European Open
5–3 QF 1991 Benson & Hedges Irish Masters

Bond wins (1)

5–2 QF 1989 BCE International

John Parrott v Tony Drago (World ranking 22)
Parrott wins (2)

5–2 Rd 4 1989 BCE International
3–1 QF 1988 Kent Cup

Drago wins (2)

6–2 Rd 3 1991 Mita World Masters
4–2 QF 1991 Canal Plus European Challenge

John Parrott v Steve Newbury (World ranking 23)
Parrott wins (1)

9–5 Rd 3 1987 UK Championship

Newbury wins (1)

5–2 Rd 4 1989 Hong Kong Open

John Parrott v Silvino Francisco (World ranking 24)
Parrott wins (1)

5–1 Rd 5 1989 Mercantile Credit Classic

Francisco wins (0)

John Parrott v Wayne Jones (World ranking 25)
Parrott wins (2)

5–3 Rd 3 1985 International
5–0 Rd 4 1990 European Open

Jones wins (1)

5–4 QF 1989 Mercantile Credit Classic

John Parrott v Joe Johnson (World ranking 26)
Parrott wins (6)

9–1 Rd 4 1986 UK Championship
9–7 QF 1988 World Matchplay
5–4 QF 1989 English Championship
5–3 QF 1990 Benson & Hedges Masters
5–2 Rd 5 1990 European Open
9–8 Rd 5 1990 UK Championship

Johnson wins (0)

Head to Head

John Parrott v Eddie Charlton (World ranking 27)
Parrott wins (2)

    5–4 Rd 5 1987 Mercantile Credit Classic
    5–1 QF 1989 European Open

Charlton wins (2)

    5–1 Rd 2 1984 Rothmans Grand Prix
    5–1 Rd 4 1991 Mercantile Credit Classic

John Parrott v Danny Fowler (World ranking 28)
Parrott wins (3)

    10–2 QRd 1985 Embassy World Championship
    10–3 QRd 4 1987 Embassy World Championship
    5–4 Rd 4 1989 English Championship

Fowler wins (0)

John Parrott v Mark Bennett (World ranking 29)
Parrott wins (1)

    10–9 Rd 1 1990 Embassy World Championship

Bennett wins (0)

John Parrott v Bob Chaperon (World ranking 30)
Parrott wins (3)

    5–1 Rd 4 1987 International
    5–2 QF 1987 Rothmans Grand Prix
    9–8 Rd 4 1989 UK Championship

Chaperon wins (0)

John Parrott v Cliff Wilson (World ranking 32)
No matches.

John Parrott v John Virgo (World ranking 31)
Parrott wins (4)

6–2 Rd 4 1985 English Championship
5–0 Rd 5 1988 Mercantile Credit Classic
5–1 Rd 4 1988 British Open
5–4 Rd 5 1988 BCE Canadian Masters

Virgo wins (1)

9–6 Rd 4 1986 English Championship

John Parrott v Darren Morgan (World ranking 33)
Parrott wins (1)

5–3 Rd 4 1988 BCE Canadian Masters

Morgan wins (1)

5–3 Rd 3 1991 European Open

John Parrott v Tony Meo (World ranking 34)
Parrott wins (7)

5–4 Rd 4 1985 International
10–4 Rd 1 1986 Embassy World Championship
10–8 Rd 1 1987 Embassy World Championship
6–2 1989 Matchroom League
16–7 SF 1989 Embassy World Championship
6–2 1990 Matchroom League
5–3 Rd 1 1990 Benson & Hedges Masters

Meo wins (3)

9–7 Rd 1 1983 UK Championship
5–3 Rd 4 1986 Rothmans Grand Prix
6–3 QF 1987 English Championship

John Parrott v Cliff Thorburn (World ranking 36)
Parrott wins (4)

  5–4 QF 1988 Benson & Hedges Masters
  7–1 1989 Matchroom League
  6–5 QF 1989 Regal Scottish Masters
  13–6 QF 1990 Embassy World Championship

Thorburn wins (4)

  9–6 Rd 4 1985 UK Championship
  5–1 Rd 1 1986 Scottish Masters
  13–10 Rd 2 1988 Embassy World Championship
  5–3 1990 Matchroom League

John Parrott v Alex Higgins (World ranking 120)
Parrott wins (4)

  5–2 Rd 1 1984 Lada Classic
  5–2 Rd 4 1987 Mercantile Credit Classic
  7–1 1989 Matchroom League
  5–4 Rd 4 1990 Mercantile Credit Classic

Higgins wins (1)

  6–4 SF 1989 Benson & Hedges Irish Masters

Career Victories
Amateur
1981 Pontin's Junior Champion 3–1 v Don Tate
1982 Pontin's Open Champion 7–4 v Ray Reardon
1982 Junior Pot Black Champion v John Keers
1983 Junior Pot Black Champion v Steve Ventham

Professional
1986 Pontin's Open Champion 7–6 v Tony Putnam
1988 Pontin's Professional Champion 9–1 v Mike Hallett

191

1989 European Open Champion (Deauville) 9–8 v Terry
   Griffiths
1990 European Open Champion (Lyon) 10–6 v Stephen Hendry
1990 Humo Belgian Masters (Antwerp) 9–6 v Jimmy White
1990 Norwich Union Grand Prix (Monaco) 4–2 v Steve Davis
1991 Embassy World Champion 18–11 v Jimmy White

Career centuries: 77 (as at 31–7–91)

Highest breaks: 142: 1990 Matchroom League.
                   140: 1990 Embassy World Championship
                   140: 1990 UK Championship

Oddities:
The only player to lead 7–0 in a World Championship final and
go on to win the title. (Steve Davis, 1985, and Eddie Charlton,
1973, both lost from this position.)

Inflicted joint heaviest World Championship defeat, 13–1,
when beating Tony Knowles in the second round.

Won the first seven frames of the final in record time, 73
minutes.

Equalled the World Championship record of eight century
breaks: 131 (v Nigel Gilbert, Rd 1); 138 (v Tony Knowles, Rd
2); 137 (v Tony Knowles, Rd 2); 101 (v Terry Griffiths, QF); 122
(v Steve Davis, SF); 117 (v Jimmy White, Final, frame 7); 112
(v Jimmy White, Final, frame 16) 112 (v Jimmy White, Final,
frame 25).

World ranking statistics
1984–85 20th. 1985–86 18th. 1986–87 17th. 1987–88 13th. 1988–
89 7th. 1989–90 2nd. 1990–91 3rd. 1991–92 4th.